"Alex McFarland is no stranger to taking on some of the toughest questions Christians face. He's done it again in this straightforward, honest, and compelling new book. Alex's personal story of finding the deep love of Christ infuses his kind yet uncompromising approach to biblical truth. He understands that if Christians want to share the Gospel effectively, we can't duck from the challenges posed by skeptics. Yet Alex addresses them with both intelligence and compassion, mindful that simply defeating false arguments will not persuade anyone, and that Jesus was filled not only with truth but also with grace (John 1:14). Alex's book is more of a conversation with a friend—a friend with a fine mind, great learning, and a deeply caring heart. Believers who care about reaching the next generation with the best news of all history will profit not only from the content of this book but by the spirit of love and hope in which it's written."

—Tony Perkins, president, Family Research Council

"Alex McFarland has done it again! Through preaching, writing, mentoring, and consulting, Alex McFarland has become a pivotal voice in the advancement of God's kingdom today. I recommend this book wholeheartedly."

—David Nasser, author, speaker, senior vice president
of Liberty University

"Myths that we believe become powerful forces that influence our thinking. Alex McFarland discloses the very personal truth that for most of his life he believed the myth that if his own earthly father couldn't love and accept him, then a perfectly holy God couldn't really want him as a son. Nothing could be further from the truth, but the myth was powerful. Whatever myths you have come to believe about Christianity or her Christ, Alex busts in this book. If you want to be set free from the lies you've been told, live into the truth offered here."

—Carmen Fowler LaBerge, president,
The Presbyterian Lay Committee

D1444529

"Once again Alex takes the truth of the Word of God and shows plainly and clearly that it is timely, relevant, and truthful to the fast-paced, changing culture of today. Each question is plainly answered with biblical truth and with the spirit of love in Christ that we all should seek to emulate."

—Carlton Gerrell, executive pastor/administrator,
Tennessee Valley Community Church, Paris, Tennessee

"It's tragic that slanderous sound bites and unsubstantiated assumptions stand in between so many people and their Creator. Thankfully, Alex McFarland is able to add clarity where there is confusion and truth where there is myth. Don't buy one, buy two—and read it together with an unbelieving friend."

—John Stonestreet, speaker and fellow,
the Chuck Colson Center for Christian Worldview;
senior content advisor, Summit Ministries

"Our buddy Alex McFarland is helping this generation understand who Jesus truly is. Through his speaking around the U.S. and in all of his books, Alex presents the truth clearly and without compromise. His new book, *The God You Thought You Knew*, is no exception. Alex gives true-life examples and application that engage the reader with every page. For those who want to be equipped to 'live loud' for Jesus, or for those who are asking themselves, 'Is all this God stuff really true?' grab a copy of this book!"

—David and Jason, The Benham Brothers

THE GOD YOU THOUGHT YOU KNEW

EXPOSING THE 10 BIGGEST MYTHS ABOUT CHRISTIANITY

ALEX McFARLAND

BETHANY HOUSE PUBLISHERS
a division of Baker Publishing Group
Minneapolis, Minnesota

Published by Bethany House Publishers
11400 Hampshire Avenue South
Bloomington, Minnesota 55438
www.bethanyhouse.com

Bethany House Publishers is a division of
Baker Publishing Group, Grand Rapids, Michigan

Printed in the United States of America

Library of Congress Cataloging-in-Publication Data
McFarland, Alex.
    The God you thought you knew : exposing the 10 biggest myths about
Christianity / Alex McFarland.
        pages cm
    Includes bibliographical references.
    Summary: "Challenges common myths and misunderstandings about
Christianity and helps readers reconsider how they think of God"— Provided
by publisher.
    ISBN 978-0-7642-1771-5 (pbk. : alk. paper)
    1. Apologetics. I. Title.
BT1100.M34 2015
239—dc23   2015016122

Cover design by LOOK Design Studio

15   16   17   18   19   20   21   7   6   5   4   3   2   1

In keeping with biblical principles of creation stewardship, Baker Publishing Group advocates the responsible use of our natural resources. As a member of the Green Press Initiative, our company uses recycled paper when possible. The text paper of this book is composed in part of post-consumer waste.

Dedicated to the one most used by God
to guide me out of myth
and into truth:

Angie

Contents

7

Acknowledgments

The main ingredient of stardom is the rest of the team.

Famed UCLA Basketball Coach
John Wooden (1910–2010)

Similar to the quotation above, there is great truth in the axiom, "No one succeeds unless a lot of other people want them to." From firsthand experience I know that this is the case. For assistance in the development of this book (and other endeavors, as well), I would like to extend heartfelt appreciation to some dedicated members of "our team":

First of all, sincere thanks are due to Andy McGuire, Ellen Chalifoux, and the wonderful staff of Baker/Bethany House publishers. I have been educated, inspired, and guided by the fine books of Baker for two and a half decades. To be writing with this exceptional Christian organization is truly a dream come true. Thank you all for working with me on this and other projects.

Special thanks also, to:

Dillon Burroughs, researcher/writer with me on many projects, who so expertly helped to format and clarify this work.

Dr. Tony Beam, vice president, North Greenville University, South Carolina. Kudos to all of our students on the school's "Life Answers Teams"! They are the upcoming apologists of this generation!

The American Family Association/American Family Radio network, including president Tim Wildmon; Wesley Wildmon; radio network manager Jim Stanley; senior vice president Buddy Smith; Randall Murphree, editor of the excellent AFA Journal; S/O to Jeff Chamblee at American Family Studios; and the entire organization. Thanks also to my faithful daily co-host on our program *Exploring the Word,* Rev. Bert Harper. Ministering with AFA/AFR has truly been life-changing for me.

Rev. Jason Jimenez, my ministry colleague in the Stand Strong Tour, ViralTruth television, and in many other projects as well.

Dr. Lawrence Clapp, my pastor at South Elm Street Baptist Church, Greensboro, North Carolina.

Dr. Mark Cowart, pastor of Church For All Nations, Colorado Springs, Colorado (a very special mentor, colleague, and friend).

Jeffrey Foskett, for thirty years a "friend who sticks closer than a brother" (Proverbs 18:24).

Michael and Debbie Hamilton and the staff of Hamilton Strategies (Hamilton is a public relations firm *par excellence;* the work they accomplish is amazing).

Stuart Epperson Jr., and the staff of Truth Broadcasting (friend and prayer partner for more than fifteen years).

Trusted friends and co-laborers Sam Hicks, T. A. Wall Jr., Neal Hughes, and our entire board at Truth For A New Generation/APCA Inc.

And thanks to the pastors, campus leaders, supporters, journalists, conference attendees, and friends with whom I interact all year long.

Most of all, I thank the Lord Jesus Christ, who loved me and gave himself for me. This work is written for his glory and honor, and ". . . that the world may believe" (John 17:21).

Introduction

As a kid, I longed to feel accepted for who I was, especially from my dad. But living on a farm in the South, I could never seem to do things right—my efforts were never satisfactory for my father. The rules seemed to always be changing. I felt as if I were constantly walking on eggshells, trying not to mess up or make him angry. Consequently, I grew up feeling rejected and believed I was never quite good enough.

I felt I needed to depend on someone or something so I could feel secure and have some stability in my life, but my home was far from a safe place. Mom and Dad fought a lot. My family was on the verge of bankruptcy and losing the family farm. With family fortunes and relationships in ruin, I sensed there was nothing I could depend on.

In addition, I longed to feel important to someone, like I mattered. My mother had drilled into me from childhood that the McFarlands were important because we descended from a long line of aristocrats and rich "grand ol' Southern land owners." But as a teenager, my sense of significance came crashing down when my dad was about to lose everything he owned.

I came to faith in Christ while in college, but my faith did little to touch my emotional needs for acceptance, security, and significance. It was not until years later that I grasped the true relational relevance of the gospel. In spring 2007 my father was in the final stages of the illness that would take his life. With our time together growing short, I longed to connect with him at a deeper level—something I had hoped for since my early childhood. Now married and living on my own, one evening I tried to share with him a little of what was happening in my life. He stared at me for the longest time and then said, "You think you're really something, don't you? But you're not. To me you're nothing but a dumb ape."

All of the rejection, insecurity, and lack of significance from my childhood came flooding back. I forced a smile, struggling to hold back the emotions I was feeling. In response, I whispered, "Well, I'm your dumb ape. And I love you."

I stood up, walked outside, and sat on the old swing in the backyard where I had grown up. For a long time that night I remained there in total darkness, feeling absolutely numb, and thought about the futility of my whole life. The one person whose affirmation I cared about most would soon pass away, yet I realized that I meant virtually nothing to him. I felt foolish and completely worthless. Silently, I wished I were the one who would soon die instead.

As I looked up at the night sky I thought, *If I've ever needed a heavenly Father to love me for who I am, it is now.* At that moment I began a quest to understand how my faith in God was meant to meet the most basic relational needs of my life, both through him and through human relationships.

In the process I discovered that my faith in Christ was not simply an idea to believe, but a truth I was to experience relationally. God had taken on the form of a human. He died so I could live in relationship with him. He did this long before I was even born, knowing I would sin and make numerous mistakes. I began to understand that I was accepted without condition. Because Christ returned to life and proved himself as Lord, I could know that his unconditional love and acceptance of me was real and I was forgiven. This also led me to know how to give and receive his unconditional acceptance in relationships with others.

I knew in my mind that God's Word was authoritative and reliable. I didn't realize that there was also an experiential truth that spoke to my need for security. This is what my insecure life was looking for—someone who had my best interests at heart and would always be there for me. Through this journey I now better understand how the alleged myths of Christianity can be addressed, both from the factual evidence that exists as well as through the offer of a secure relationship of unconditional love. As we walk through these pages together, it is my great hope that you will experience a similar transformation in your own life and be anchored in a deep, lasting relationship with God.

Jesus Loves Me—At Least I Think He Does

"Jesus loves me, this I know, for the Bible tells me so." I sang these words before I even knew what they meant. I would later also learn the popular verse from John 3:16: "For God so loved the world that he gave his one and only Son." But from Monday through Saturday, the example I experienced gave me reason to wonder whether I was loved for who I was or for what I did.

Growing up on a farm meant one thing—hard work. There were always animals to feed, fields to work, and equipment to repair. My dad rose before the sun and worked until after it set. He expected no less from me. My days at home consisted of a schedule more demanding than most pre-season football practices, all in an effort to teach me the importance and value of a "good day's work."

While I am thankful for these experiences in many ways, the message they sent had a negative effect on my understanding of God. *If God is a father,* I thought, *then he must operate a lot like my father.* This worldview would lead me to deal with God like a good negotiator. I would perform some good actions to cover up my bad behaviors. If I felt like I was messing up too much (which was often), I would work harder at performing better—reading the Bible, saying a prayer at church, volunteering for a service project. In my mind it made sense. Keep God happy and things will turn out all right.

By college I realized the faulty logic of this approach. No matter how many good things I tried to accomplish, they would never be enough to cover my growing list of shortcomings. I wasn't partying hard and dropping out of school; I had simply lived long enough to realize I wasn't good enough to keep God happy in my own strength. My options were either to stop trying or to find some other way to please God.

Through the influence of some college friends, I finally came to understand the true Good News of Jesus. Rather than earning God's approval, I discovered that I could accept the salvation he had provided as a free gift. I didn't have to earn a spot at the table; the table had already been set. Instead, I was called to believe in Christ. When I did, I was given a new life.

I wish I could say everything changed about my view of God at that moment. The truth is that my view of who he is and how he operates has taken years to develop. At that time, I realized God loved me and offered me new life as a gift; what I didn't realize was how big this gift was. It wasn't merely about a ticket to heaven; it included a transformed life, one where I could find unconditional acceptance in him.

Receiving His Love

It has been said that the greatest lessons you learn often come through the deepest pains you experience. This has certainly been my case. Shortly after becoming a follower of Christ, I graduated college at the nearby University of North Carolina at Greensboro and entered graduate school at a Christian college to prepare for ministry. This was not a popular move in my home, as my father expected me to return after college to help run the family business.

Instead of returning home, I ran about as far in the other direction as possible. Following my seminary graduation, I felt led to take on an unprecedented challenge. I would become the first minister to preach in all fifty states in fifty days. This "Tour of Truth" across America included sixty-four evangelistic services, became the subject of my first book, and was used by God to bring many people to personal faith in Christ.

Part of me thought my parents would finally accept my new calling and celebrate my accomplishments. When they didn't, the feelings of joy disappeared. Why couldn't I make my parents happy?

Looking back, this may have been part of my motivation to prove myself in the following years. I served at one of the largest Christian ministries in the nation, spoke at more than fourteen hundred churches and events, published more than a hundred articles and a dozen books, and started a nationwide radio and television program. At one time, I even served as president of a Christian seminary, a position few had obtained at such an early age.

Though successful from a ministry standpoint, I began to realize my relationship with God was more transactional than unconditional. In other words, I unintentionally sought God's approval by how hard I worked and performed for him. The same way I sought to earn my father's approval simply transitioned to earning God's favor. Though I had accepted his gift of eternal life by faith, I was too often living like it depended on me.

It was during this time that God revealed a new understanding of his love for me. Rather than earning his love, I was simply to receive it. My attitude began to shift from earning to receiving. The example of John the Baptist became a personal theme during this time. When asked about the growing popularity of Jesus over his own ministry, John responded, "A person can receive only what is given them from heaven" (John 3:27).

In short, God clearly taught me ministry is not achieved; ministry is received.

Just as I did nothing to earn eternal life, I can do nothing to make God love me any more or any less. I am already perfectly loved, accepted, forgiven, and redeemed. Though I had read these truths repeatedly over the years, it was as if God had removed the blinders from my eyes to see his perspective on this issue.

Words of Love

When I pause to reflect on God's words about love, I find promises like:

> God demonstrates his own love for us in this: While we were still sinners, Christ died for us.
>
> Romans 5:8

> For I am convinced that neither death nor life, neither angels nor demons, neither the present nor the future, nor any powers, neither height nor depth, nor anything else in all creation, will be able to separate us from the love of God that is in Christ Jesus our Lord.
>
> Romans 8:38–39

See what great love the Father has lavished on us, that we should be called children of God!

1 John 3:1

This is how we know what love is: Jesus Christ laid down his life for us.

1 John 3:16

Love comes from God.

1 John 4:7

We love because he first loved us.

1 John 4:19

This love is perfect and unconditional. God loved us before our creation, during our sins, and despite our ongoing failures. In one of my previous books, I noted how God accepts us without condition:

> The prostitutes, tax collectors, and beggars . . . all those considered the low-lifes whom everyone shunned were in fact the ones Jesus hung out with the most. The gospel message clearly proves that it doesn't matter what your past is or how badly you've messed up, because Jesus' love extends beyond measure. In His loving eyes, you are welcomed and accepted.[1]

Finding Acceptance in the Right Places

When singer Amy Winehouse tragically died due to alcohol poisoning, the story attracted the attention of millions of Americans. Amy was an award-winning celebrity who enjoyed praise from fans, respect from critics, and international fame. But clearly the perks of stardom and the gratification of artistic expression aren't enough to fill the human heart. When public figures self-destruct it is a vivid reminder that beginning as early in life as possible, individuals need to develop healthy perspectives on their value as human beings.

Amy Winehouse had quietly become part of a group of performers that some call "Club 27." These musical talents partied hard, burned out early, and died at age twenty-seven (including Jimi Hendrix, Janis Joplin, Jim Morrison, and Kurt Cobain). Winehouse seemed to truly be on a path of intentional destruction. Her journey included alcoholism, drug use, and shocking changes in appearance. She had many successes that people would assume should amount to happiness—yet it was clear she remained unfulfilled.

> "Fame is a vapor, popularity an accident, and riches take wings. Only one thing endures, and that is character."
>
> Horace Greeley (1811–1872), newspaper publisher, journalist, one-time presidential candidate

Such celebrity passings can serve as an opportunity to discuss some of the basic realities regarding what it means to be human. Though they may not say it in these words, all people seek acceptance, significance, and security. We all want to feel like we have value as people and that our lives have meaning. Our pursuits of solid answers to the heart's deep longings may tempt us toward actions that can be harmful. The quest to fill the heart can lead to destruction of the body and soul.

After working with countless people through two decades of ministry, I have interacted with many who have worn themselves down and burned themselves out because they did not know their true worth. I believe it is important for people of all ages to find personal worth, value, and meaning in appropriate places. The natural longings of the human mind and soul should be answered in ways that are beneficial to the individual.

For those who follow Christ, there are clear and tangible reasons to feel accepted. Our understanding of our personal worth is built upon several biblical principles:

1. We are created in God's image;
2. Jesus personally cares about us;
3. We are part of a family of people who follow Christ (the church);
4. Our citizenship and future residence are in heaven; and
5. God has a perfect purpose and plan for our lives.

These truths can offer great encouragement, but we realize emotions don't automatically "catch up" to the facts we hold in our mind. Self-esteem issues often feed on irrationality. We must vigilantly pursue an honest view of ourselves, our circumstances, and God. Feelings of insecurity (which can lead to unhealthy behaviors) should not overpower the facts (that we are made in God's image and are complete in Christ).

Of the five realities listed above, none lead us to find our value by comparing our lives to others'. Someone else will always come along who is more attractive, is a better athlete, has more money, has a higher GPA, drives a nicer car, or owns a bigger home. If we approach life as a competition, it doesn't take long to realize we eventually get left in the dust of the next fastest runner. Instead, we find our comfort in the acceptance that comes from Christ.

Tragic deaths like that of Amy Winehouse act as reminders that people of all ages need a clear understanding of who God is and a personal experience of his love and compassion. This provides lasting purpose and clear direction even during the most difficult moments of life.

The Journey of a Thousand Miles . . .

It has been said that the journey of a thousand miles begins with a single step. I pray that the pages in this book will help bring you several steps closer to God. In our time together, we'll look at ten common myths I have observed in communicating with audiences around the world for the past two decades. These persistent ideas continue to rob both believers and seekers—whether young or old, regardless of ethnicity or economics—of an authentic relationship with God. We'll discover that each of these myths contain a grain of truth yet also involve a level of deception that blurs the vision of what God intends for our lives. Together, we'll walk through the biblical and practical ways these myths can be overcome with truth and applied in our own lives and among those around us.

Let me warn you now: The words you read will challenge your assumptions about God and the Bible. I encourage you to be open to a new way of thinking. When we fully grasp the kind of life God offers, we'll find ourselves convicted, motivated, and encouraged to live fully devoted to him. May God bless you as you seek the truth!

Myth #1

Christianity is intolerant and judgmental toward others

Truth: Christianity teaches to love neighbor as self and to share the love of Jesus with others

Even though Mahatma Gandhi had studied the Bible and met many Christians, he rejected Christianity in large part because he wasn't impressed with Christians. "I like your Christ," he is reported to have said, "but I do not like your Christians. Your Christians are so unlike your Christ."[1] Christians *can* be intolerant and judgmental. But as I ask in my book *The 21 Toughest Questions Your Kids Will Ask You About Christianity,*

> Is the bad behavior of Christians enough to warrant rejection of Jesus as Savior? I would argue no. The person who rejects Christian hypocrisy is aware that there is a missed mark, which is sin. The fact that there are sinners in the world should point to a need for Christ and his redemption—not the opposite. [You

are free to make a] decision about Jesus and salvation. But the basis of that decision should be an examination of the life of Jesus and His teachings, not the sometimes-disappointing lives of His followers.[2]

Are Christians Really Intolerant and Judgmental?

The statement that Christians are intolerant is commonly made when a Christian individual or group objects to a truth claim that contradicts a Christian truth claim. Many today consider truth to be relative and label those who claim that truth is objective as intolerant. However, this is a misunderstanding of intolerance. To be intolerant requires more than denying the truth of an opposing truth claim. Intolerance also requires action of some sort. Disagreement alone is not intolerance.

Second, this view assumes that peace and love are incompatible with intolerance. However, there are many examples where the promotion of peace and love is compatible with intolerance. Take the case of a misbehaving child, particularly a child whose behavior might cause harm to himself or a sibling. The parent will not tolerate the misbehavior and will discipline the child. The discipline administered stems from love for the child and the desire to correct his behavior, bringing about greater peace and safety within the family. The promotion of peace and love is not inherently incompatible with being intolerant.

Other examples can be found throughout history. In the African-American Civil Rights movement, Martin Luther King Jr. encouraged nonviolent protest to promote change in American society regarding segregation and civil rights. He was intolerant of racism and segregation yet promoted his views through peace and nonviolence. He followed both the nonviolent principles of Gandhi that had been practiced in India as well as the nonviolent methods used by Jesus and his followers to spread the Good News.

Sharing and defending the truth of the Gospel may at times be disagreeable. But it is not intolerant and, unless sin in the believer's life results in another motivation, it is done out of love for the unbeliever. While Christianity does defend certain moral standards, biblically informed moral boundaries have contributed much good to the human condition. In a culture where biblical values are diminished, the issue

> "By this everyone will know that you are my disciples, if you love one another."
>
> John 13:35

is not, Will there be moral values in a culture? The real question is, Which values will drive our culture?

Christianity has often been labeled intolerant and judgmental, but is this an accurate view of Christ's life and teachings? When asked, "What is the greatest commandment?" Jesus responded: "'Love the Lord your God with all your heart and with all your soul and with all your mind.' This is the first and greatest commandment. And the second is like it: 'Love your neighbor as yourself'" (Matthew 22:37–39).

Jesus taught love for God and love for others as the most important teachings of the faith. While not every Christian faithfully applies these principles, many do. Christianity presents a faith based on love, concern for others, and making a difference in this world that will impact eternity.

Hot Topic: Why Do Christians Judge Gay People?

If the Bible teaches that Christians are to love other people, then why do Christians judge gay people? This is the concern of many I have spoken with over the years. A biblical view would state that if a Christian truly loves everyone—even someone who is gay—he or she will treat everyone with respect and dignity

25

regardless of a person's beliefs or actions. And Christians believe that the most caring act they can do is to help someone come to faith in Jesus Christ and live for him.

Homosexual activity, as well as any form of sexual activity outside of marriage between a man and woman, is condemned in the Bible's teachings. As a result, Christians are called to help people move away from sexual activities contrary to God's will and help them pursue purity in their walk with him. What is more loving—to let someone live however they choose, or to help them pursue what is best for their life? This is the challenge Christians face in their efforts to share the Good News of Jesus with those who are gay.

To be fair, Christians vary greatly in their response to this topic. Those who treat gay individuals with hatred or violence clearly violate the biblical teaching to speak the truth in love (Ephesians 4:15). Other believers, however, have failed to speak truth in their desire not to offend. Rather than speak the truth when inconvenient, a growing number of Christians have chosen to remain silent or to even support gay relationships. Neither is appropriate for those who seek to follow Christ.

How did Jesus respond to homosexuality? Some argue that Jesus never spoke against it and gave no opinion on the matter. This is only partially accurate. Jesus did speak clearly about marriage and sexuality in his teachings about divorce in Matthew 19:4–6:

> At the beginning the Creator "made them male and female," and said, "For this reason a man will leave his father and mother and be united to his wife, and the two will become one flesh" . . .
> So they are no longer two, but one flesh. Therefore what God has joined together, let no one separate.

In these words, Jesus clearly ruled out sexuality of all kinds outside of marriage between a man and woman.

Notice, however, what was not said. Jesus did not speak frequently about sexuality or homosexuality. He did not single out homosexual activity as a bigger wrong than any other. He instead came to seek and to save the lost, to serve rather than to be served, and to give his life for the sins of all people.

> "Whatever a person may be like, we must still love them because we love God."
>
> John Calvin (1509–1564)

When we realize Christ's approach to sexuality, we discover that he does not limit our desires or make us feel badly about ourselves; rather, he wants us to live fully for him and according to his ways.

Why Are Christians So Hypocritical?

One of the most popular Bible verses of this generation is Matthew 7:1: "Do not judge, or you too will be judged." No one wants to be told his or her way is wrong. When Christians condemn the actions of others, whether in a kind manner or not, they are seen as hypocritical rather than helpful.

What is the proper response? The following verse in Matthew 7:2–5, often neglected by those who discourage the judgment of others, offers a helpful corrective:

> For in the same way you judge others, you will be judged, and with the measure you use, it will be measured to you.
>
> Why do you look at the speck of sawdust in your brother's eye and pay no attention to the plank in your own eye? How can you say to your brother, "Let me take the speck out of your eye," when all the time there is a plank in your own eye? You hypocrite, first take the plank out of your own eye, and then you will see clearly to remove the speck from your brother's eye.

Christians are not perfect, just forgiven. The proper response to the sins of others begins with a close examination of our own lives. Do we hear the words of God yet fail to live them? If so, we "merely listen to the word, and so deceive ourselves" (James 1:22). Instead, we are called to live humbly before the Lord and then seek to help others in need.

The Bible says that all people are sinners. We are sinners by birth (Psalm 51:5). But we are also sinners by choice, because we know what's right yet often do what's wrong (James 4:17). In the day that we all stand before God, the Bible says each person's conscience will either accuse or excuse him (Romans 2:15–16). The ultimate questions are not, "Have I lived a perfect life?" or, "Was I ever hypocritical?" They are, "What did I do with Jesus?" and, "What was my response to God's offer of forgiveness through his Son?"

Because everyone at times acts as a hypocrite, this objection is simply an attack against hypocrisy. It says nothing about the truth or falsity of Christian truth claims—except to reinforce the idea that everyone has sinned. The unfortunate fact that Christians are sometimes hypocritical says nothing about whether or not God exists, whether the Bible is true, or if Jesus is God's Son. The Christian faith does not rest upon the validity of its messengers; it rests upon the validity of its message.

Why Do Christians Think They're Right and Others Are Wrong?

The number-one thing that sets Christianity apart from other religions is that Christianity offers a relationship with a living, death-conquering Savior. In other words, our God is alive.

When Christians claim the Bible's content has been preserved and remains unchanged through the centuries or that Jesus Christ was crucified two thousand years ago during Passover and rose from the grave, it's much more than personal opinion. Christianity is a belief system offering objective truth.

28

Christianity does not ask people to give their lives for human opinion. Additionally, Christians are people who have experienced a relationship with the person who said he was the personification of truth.

Christians, like followers of other belief systems, think their teachings are true. But contradictory truth claims cannot both be correct at the same time. For instance, Christians say that Jesus was crucified, and Muslims say that Jesus was not crucified. It cannot be true that Jesus both was crucified and was not crucified. One or the other view must be incorrect.

Jesus said that no one could come to God but through him (John 14:6). Was Jesus right about this, or was he wrong? He could not both be the Savior and also not be the Savior. Either he was or he wasn't. The point is that Christians do not insist that their beliefs are true out of pride or stubbornness, but based on their understanding of Scripture.

Christians believe that their faith is reasonable based on compelling evidence that accompanies the claims. Christian convictions can be examined, tested, empirically investigated, and evaluated for their plausibility. In other words, Christianity claims to be objectively true. For example, the cities of the Bible's events are all real cities, many of which can still be visited today. The city of Bethlehem, where Jesus was born, still exists. The city of Hebron, the resting place of Abraham from the book of Genesis, is still inhabited in the twenty-first century.

In these and many other biblical accounts, the teachings are based on real locations involving local customs and languages that match the time and place in which events occurred. When skeptics speak of Jesus in the same sentence as the Easter Bunny or tooth fairy, they make an inaccurate connection between myth and reality. Christianity affirms the miraculous, yet it is also deeply rooted in history and reality.

Isn't Christianity the Same as Other Religions?

One of the illustrations often used to make the point that all religious beliefs are basically the same and will result in the same destination is the story of the blind men and the elephant. The story is told with some variations, but the basic account is that a group of blind men are examining an elephant. Each blind man grasps a different part of the elephant, such as the tusks, the tail, or an ear. They each then give a different explanation for the reality they experience. One says that the elephant is like a wall; another says it's like a rope. We are supposed to then be surprised by the simple wisdom of the solution—they are all right! Similarly, we're told, even though there are many ways to express religious beliefs and worldviews, we're all simply grasping different parts of the one, unified reality around us. We are then supposed to realize how foolish we've been by pursuing so many different and seemingly incompatible beliefs, when in reality we're all right.

> "As Christians, we practice tolerance in the classical sense of the word and allow others to hold to their beliefs with which we disagree. We do not threaten or harm them in any way, but all the while we seek to show them that Christianity is true and people everywhere need Jesus for the forgiveness of their sins."
>
> Apologist Jacob Allee

But does the story of the blind men and the elephant really support the view that all religions teach the same basic message? Not if we investigate carefully. First, the person telling the story is essentially claiming that the different points of view, as expressed by many different religions, are wrong, and that the only one with the real answer is the person telling the story. That doesn't seem quite right, does it? There was an objective truth to be grasped—the elephant—that the blind men all failed to apprehend. In other words, they were all wrong about the true reality before them. Following this line of reasoning, we could say that worldviews may grasp some aspects of the truth about reality but fail to grasp the entirety of reality. Buddhists, then, may be right about life and suffering basically being the same, as we all experience pain and suffering, but they may be wrong about the nature of human beings and the nature of salvation. Each person touching the elephant may grasp some truth, yet this example uses an imperfect elephant as the basis for judgment. If an all-powerful God exists, he could reveal more than one piece of himself to those who seek him. In fact, both Christ and Scripture reveal truth about God that are far superior than the example given of the elephant.

Another popular illustration that is supposed to validate the idea of all religions being equal is the story of the paths up to the top of a mountain. The plot of this story concerns the fact that there is more than one path to the top of a mountain. Similarly, there are many paths that will lead to spiritual freedom. To claim there is only one path is not only false but narrow-minded and intolerant. What kind of God would do this? "Of course," we're supposed to respond, "how could I have been so foolish! There are many paths to the top of a mountain."

What's wrong with the mountain illustration? First, it's a false analogy. Grasping metaphysical truth is not the same thing as climbing a mountain, no more than coming to the solution of a math problem is like getting to the top of a mountain. Sure, we might go about our solution to a math problem in different ways, but in the end there is only one true answer to the question. Is it narrow-minded to say that two plus two is four and only four? Or is it merely an objective statement of the truth? If we're on the wrong path when it comes to spiritual truths regarding reality, the best choice is to join the right path.

Many people believe that Judaism, Christianity, and Islam teach the same basic things. While all three of these Abrahamic faiths share a view of one God, there are far more differences than similarities. They all have different teachings about God, salvation, life's purpose, and the afterlife.

Boston University Professor Stephen R. Prothero documented this fact clearly in his bestselling book *God Is Not One*. Prothero examined eight major world religions, noting that their core teachings are in fact *very dissimilar*.

For example, Hinduism includes many gods, while Christianity has only one. Hindu gods are said to bring peace and to fight against evil spirits. Its scriptures claim 330 million gods exist, emanating as extensions of the one force, Brahman. The most important Hindu gods include Brahman, Brahma, Vishnu, and Shiva. Brahman is considered impersonal and unknowable. Lesser deities are understood as having their own attributes and abilities but are seen as products of Brahman. Brahman alone exists, with all else ultimately being *maya* or an illusion. Does this sound compatible with the teachings of other religions?

In contrast, atheism teaches there is no God. Wicca believes in a god and a goddess. Buddhism sees the universe as one rather than identifying a list of many gods. Other religious movements blend the ideas of one or more religions into additional belief systems. All of these religions cannot be true when they hold to divergent viewpoints on the identity of their very deity.

Another key area of difference involves authoritative writings. In Christianity, the Old and New Testament writings found in the Bible are considered the authoritative works used as the basis for the faith's teachings. Islam uses an entirely different book—the Qur'an—as its authoritative source. Judaism follows only the teachings of the Old Testament that they call the Hebrew Bible. Because each religion follows a different authoritative book, each religion's teachings include a wide range of differing interpretations.

For instance, Islam teaches that salvation is based on works, while Christianity teaches that salvation comes from faith in

Jesus alone. One of the main dividing points between the three Abrahamic religions is that they disagree in their teachings about who Jesus was. Judaism does not recognize Jesus as the Messiah that God had promised his people. Islam teaches that Jesus was just a prophet, nothing more. Jesus, however, claimed to be "the way and the truth and the life" in John 14:6. After making that claim, Jesus added, "No one comes to the Father except through me."

This is precisely what Christianity teaches: that no one can come to God except through Jesus Christ. This belief separates Christianity from Judaism and Islam because Christianity is the only religion that teaches that belief in Jesus is necessary for salvation. All other religions fail to recognize Jesus' claim to be the only path to God. Jesus' resurrection from the dead proved that he is indeed God and confirmed that what he taught is true: Jesus is the only way to God. Similarity does not equal sameness.

Truth Matters

In John 18:38, Pilate asked Jesus the question "What is truth?" At least five essential facts about truth can be known and discussed that are important for addressing the myth that Christians are intolerant and judgmental. They include:

1. Truth exists.
2. Truth can be known.
3. Truth connects with reality.
4. Truth can be communicated.
5. Truth is personally important.

First, truth exists. In contrast with the postmodern worldview that claims truth is relative, Christianity includes a worldview in which objective truth exists. In fact, to claim that truth does not exist is to make a truth claim. There is no escaping that certain realities do exist and must be addressed. Some of these realities include life and death, morality, and our ultimate purpose.

Second, truth can be known. We can observe nature to better understand the truth of the physical world. Science provides an academic look at this observational approach to truth in the natural realm. In the spiritual realm, Jesus claimed to be the way, the truth, and the life (John 14:6). The Bible claims that there are not many ways to know God, but only one, and that there are not many gods and goddesses with the choice given to us regarding which ones to follow or whether to follow any at all; God is one (Deuteronomy 6:4–5).

> "Religion's misdeeds may make for provocative history, but the everyday good works of billions of people is the real history of religion, one that parallels the growth and prosperity of humankind. There are countless examples of individuals lifting themselves out of personal misery through faith. In the lives of these individuals, God is not a delusion, God is not a spell that must be broken—God is indeed great."[3]
>
> Bruce Sheiman, *An Atheist Defends Religion*

In contrast, some suggest beliefs about truth and morality are based on personal preference, cultural conditioning, or religious background. In other words, there are no absolute moral rights or wrongs. While there are many cultures worldwide, there is also a universal sense of morality, or right and wrong, found in every culture of the world. While many theologians use this observation to point to the reality of God's existence (known as the moral argument), it is also important to note that this universal sense of morality includes many similar moral beliefs. Laws against murder, theft, and other offenses suggest there are universal truths regarding morality as well as truths about the physical world.

Third, truth connects with reality. Truth is not merely "out there" somewhere to be discovered; it is embedded in the reality around us. What does this mean? In some Eastern religions, it is claimed that this world is an illusion. To find the truth or true reality, one must meditate and seek the truth that can be found in an enlightened state. But this is only partially accurate. While we can meditate on the truths of God, there is no escaping the reality around us. The car you drive is not an illusion; it is real. The people close to you in your life are not illusions; they are real people you care about and who care about you. Truth connects with the reality around us. We may not always understand it accurately, but it does exist and includes purpose and meaning.

Truth is also not something we create, but something we seek. We don't get to wake up one morning and say, "London is the capital of the United States." No one will accept your postmodern perspective if you say, "Washington, D.C., as the capital of the United States is truth for you, but not for me. I prefer London." Why not? London is not even located in the United States, and the U.S. already has its own capital city: Washington, D.C. As a child, you learn the truth about the capital of the nation; you don't get to choose your own. While there are many areas of life in which we can choose our preferences, there are other areas in which truth exists. When we blur this distinction, we can find ourselves looking foolish when we realize there is an objective truth in an area we considered a preference or choice.

Fourth, truth can be communicated. The letters, words, and paragraphs on this page have meaning that is intended to communicate ideas to help you as a reader. Likewise, the Bible also communicates truth to assist us in our spiritual lives. People can debate whether it is true or accurate (we will discuss this in detail in a later chapter), but the Bible is clearly a book written to communicate truth to those who seek to follow Jesus.

Fifth, truth is personally important. A warning sign that says *Poison* on a bottle can save your life, but only when you read and obey it. When the bottle is on the shelf at a store, the truth that it includes poison is unimportant to you. However, when you hold the bottle in your hand, the decision regarding how to use it becomes personally important. It can be used for its intended, helpful purpose, or it can be used in a harmful manner. Truth has implications and consequences in our lives, sometimes even involving situations of life and death.

I joke that we like to say truth is relative when it comes to matters of faith, but we would never make such a claim when the consequences are negative to our own lives. If a doctor told you that you were facing cancer, you would want to know how to defeat it. You would not be satisfied if he responded, "Just take whatever medicine you want; they're all the same," or if he said, "The operation doesn't matter. You can pick the one you like best." We know medical operations are not a game! They can be a matter of life or death.

The same is true spiritually. If we want to know how to live beyond this life and to enjoy a life of purpose and meaning today, we must seek the truth regarding the matter. It is not an issue of personal choice or preference. It is not intolerant or judgmental to seek what is right and to communicate it to others. The truth is what we search for, savor, and share to help others.

Building Bridges to Share the Good News

The late Dr. Jerry Falwell founded Liberty University and served as pastor of Thomas Road Baptist Church in Lynchburg, Virginia. Larry Flynt is the publisher of *Hustler* magazine. Both men were known for speaking their minds. Falwell's son, Jonathan, recalls what happened after a debate between his father and Flynt:

Mr. Flynt asked my dad if we could give him a ride back to Lynchburg in my dad's private jet. Dad said yes, so we traveled to the airport and boarded a beautiful black-and-gold Gulfstream III. As we flew to Virginia, I sat across from Dad and Mr. Flynt as they had a long conversation about sports, food, politics, and other ordinary topics. I was amazed and bewildered because they kept talking like old friends.

After we dropped off Mr. Flynt in Lynchburg, I asked Dad, "How come you could sit on that airplane and carry on a conversation with Larry Flynt as if you guys were lifelong buddies? Dad, he's the exact opposite of everything you believe in; he does all the things you preach against; and yet you were treating him like a member of your own church. Why?"

Dad's response changed my whole outlook on ministry. "Jonathan," he said, "there's going to be a day when Larry is hurting and lonely, and he'll be looking for help and guidance. He is going to pick up the phone and call someone who can help him. I want to earn the right to be that phone call!"[4]

Dr. Falwell employed a significant principle in his dealings with Mr. Flynt: In order to earn the right to share our viewpoint with others, we have to build bridges rather than burn them. Sincere followers of Jesus are not intolerant and judgmental.

Myth #2

Christianity cannot be true because of the evil and suffering in our world

Truth: Christianity offers the best hope and power to deal with suffering

Is it possible for a good God to exist and yet allow the evil and suffering that occurs in our world? This question may be the number-one barrier for those who reject Christianity. A perfect Creator and a world filled with both natural disasters and moral evil appear to be two irreconcilable concepts. Yet the problem of evil is not the end of Christianity. Christianity offers the best hope and power to deal with suffering.

World religions have long sought to address and answer the problem of evil. Overall, five responses have emerged. **The first option is atheism.** The atheist believes there is no God and therefore evil can exist because God does not.

The second option is called dualism. This worldview suggests that evil and good are really the same thing—yin and yang, simply two sides of the same coin.

The third option is illusionism. Common in Eastern religions, illusionism is the belief that what we view as evil is instead merely *maya* or an illusion. The way to escape this illusion is typically through meditation in efforts to reach enlightenment.

A fourth option is finite theism. This view believes that a God exists, but not a deity who is all powerful and all good. Instead, God has limits. Either evil is part of his character, or he is not evil but is simply not all powerful and is unable to stop the evil found in our world.

The fifth option is the biblical view of God. Christianity teaches that God is all powerful and wise and that evil is real. However, evil is limited and will not exist in our lives forever. God has already addressed the problem of evil through Jesus Christ and will one day create a new heaven and earth in which there is no evil.

The Nature of Evil

Before we dive into the details of the problem of evil, it will help to have some background information. Specifically, we want to ask at least two questions: (1) What is evil? and (2) What kinds of evil exist? We may not be able to offer a textbook definition of evil, but it's one of those things we seem to instinctively recognize: We know it when we see it.

One good thing about approaching topics like evil and suffering today is the fact that we have some two thousand years of Christian history and thought to look back on. Fortunately for us, our Christian brothers and sisters from ages past weren't idle when it came to trying to understand issues like evil and suffering. As an example, one popular approach to evil found in the writings of Augustine claims that evil is not an actual thing but is in fact a privation. What is a privation? A privation is something good that is missing. Dr. Winfried Corduan, professor of philosophy and religion, explains this approach this way:

> I am carrying an umbrella on a rainy day. By and large the umbrella does a fair job of keeping the water off my head; that is good. However, there is a hole in the umbrella; that is evil. For our purposes, the question is, what does this evil consist of? The evil lies, not in the presence of something extra, but in the absence of something that should be there but is not, namely umbrella material. . . . *Evil is the absence of good*. Philosophers prefer to speak of *the privation of good*.[1]

What Kinds of Evil Exist?

Another matter to consider is the kinds of evil that exist. Take a moment and think about evil. What comes to mind? I'm guessing at least part of what you thought of included what we'll call moral evil—evil that people do to one another. In fact, this is the primary sort of evil we encounter on a regular basis, especially as we watch the news on TV or online. People do a lot of harm to one another. They rob banks, shoot one another, hit one another, commit acts of terrorism, and more. If this sort of moral evil teaches us anything, it should be that human beings are *not* good by nature. This is no surprise to readers of the Bible, which recognizes that human beings are in a bad state and, therefore, are in need of some real redemption.

What other kinds of evil came to your mind? Maybe you also flashed back to memories of natural disasters, many of which have caused a lot of pain and suffering. From hurricanes to earthquakes to floods, natural disasters are a regular occurrence in our world. We can't say these are exclusively God's judgment, because such natural disasters often strike Christians, too. Unlike moral evil, which human beings do to one another, natural evil refers to these sorts of events. Do Christian explanations of evil take natural evil into consideration? Sometimes, but in most instances we tend to try to find explanations for moral evils.

Where Did Evil Originate?

The word *evil* first appears in the Bible in Genesis 2:17: "You must not eat from the tree of the knowledge of good and evil, for when you eat from it you will certainly die." God created humans with the ability to choose good and evil. When they did, sin entered the world, as did judgment (Genesis 3). This judgment also extended to the serpent, Satan, the one who deceived humanity and continues to do so.

Notice that evil did not originate from God. Humans sinned as the result of listening to the lie of Satan. Satan was one of God's created beings, yet one who turned to evil and brought it to humanity. God did not create evil, but he did create a universe in which evil could exist, including humans with the ability to choose good or evil.

As the result of Adam and Eve's disobedience, sin passed on to the rest of humanity (Romans 3:23). Theologians call this the sin nature. Many think of evil people as drug dealers or terrorists, but the Bible is clear that every person has a sin nature and sins in life. The penalty the Bible describes for these sins is death (Romans 6:23).

Why Didn't God Stop Evil?

If God knows everything, he knew how much suffering would eventually come into this world. Why didn't he stop this process before it all got started, and save us from all of the pain we would face? This line of questioning assumes it is possible for God to know what will happen and that he must do something to prevent it from happening. If God is loving and hates evil, wouldn't he keep it from happening in the first place? These two areas seem incompatible.

> "I have told you these things, so that in me you may have peace. In this world you will have trouble. But take heart! I have overcome the world."
>
> Jesus (John 16:33)

A better question would be, "If God knew what would happen if he created everything the way it is, why did he do it?" This assumes that there are truths about what creatures would freely do if placed in certain circumstances. If there are, then God is constrained by what those truths happen to be, and for all we know, this may be the best world that could be, given what those truths in fact turned out to be. If there aren't such truths, then God can hardly be held responsible for not acting on the basis of them.

When discussing such matters, theologians and philosophers often talk about "the best of all possible worlds" God could have created. But most Christian thinkers assert that our realm of existence, with all the details as they are, is "the only possible world." Let's again look at the facts as we have them: God created humans who were initially perfect, yet with free will (and therefore the capacity to disobey and sin). It would have been a contradiction for God to create free creatures who weren't free.

In order to act in accord with his own nature (his holiness, righteousness, truth, love, justice) and to act within the parameters of what is logical and reasonable, God created the universe as it is. God populated this universe with creatures as they are. Someone will point out that, in its current fallen condition, the world we live in is not "the best of all possible worlds." This is true. But God's plan of redemption and universal restoration is in process (the empty tomb is proof of Christ's victory over sin and death), and that plan will culminate in the restoration of righteousness throughout the created order. You could say it is "the best way to the best of all possible worlds." In light of all the known facts, the world could be no other way than the way it is.

Lost in the Weeds?

Jesus told a story known as the Parable of the Weeds, which expresses God's patience and plans regarding sin and evil. In Matthew 13:24–30 Jesus said:

> The kingdom of heaven is like a man who sowed good seed in his field. But while everyone was sleeping, his enemy came and sowed weeds among the wheat, and went away. When the wheat sprouted and formed heads, then the weeds also appeared.
>
> The owner's servants came to him and said, "Sir, didn't you sow good seed in your field? Where then did the weeds come from?"
>
> "An enemy did this," he replied.
>
> The servants asked him, "Do you want us to go and pull them up?"
>
> "No," he answered, "because while you are pulling the weeds, you may uproot the wheat with them. Let both grow together until the harvest. At that time I will tell the harvesters: First collect the weeds and tie them in bundles to be burned; then gather the wheat and bring it into my barn."

God allows moral evil to exist due to his patience. He longs for many to turn to him in faith before the time is too late. However, his patience is limited and evil will one day be judged. Delayed justice is much different from injustice.

If this were the end of the story, it would indeed be a tragedy. Thankfully, God does have a plan to eradicate evil. The final phase will include his re-creation of the world as described in the final chapters of Revelation. But long before this time, God took the ultimate step of providing an answer to evil through sending Jesus Christ to our world in earthly form. First Corinthians 15:45 shares that Jesus is humanity's second chance: "'The first man Adam became a living being'; the last Adam [Jesus], a life-giving spirit."

Why Evil Persists

Why does evil continue to persist today? Romans 3:25 notes,

> God presented Christ as a sacrifice of atonement, through the shedding of his blood—to be received by faith. He did this to demonstrate his righteousness, because in his forbearance he had left the sins committed beforehand unpunished.

Jesus Christ paid the price for our sins. The sacrifices of the Jews in the tabernacle and temple were temporary. With the death and resurrection of Jesus, the perfect sacrifice, there was no longer need for further offerings. As Hebrews 10:10 states, "We have been made holy through the sacrifice of the body of Jesus Christ once and for all."

Interestingly, those who admit there is evil in our world acknowledge the existence of right and wrong, moral absolutes that point toward an ultimate moral lawgiver, or God. God is the Creator, Sustainer, and basis of all ultimate morality. In a universe with no ultimate standards of good and evil, there could be no way to define right and wrong. The Bible's message from the beginning is that the world was created as "good." Yet evil persists. Why does God allow bad things to happen?

Natural evil exists because our world is subject to decay and death. Romans 8:21 notes, "Creation itself will be liberated from its bondage to decay and brought into the freedom and glory of the children of God."

Think about the weather patterns we see on a daily basis and how these might be connected to our disobedience. Following the judgment of Adam and Eve's sin in the Garden of Eden, evil continued to grow in the lives of people. By the time of Noah, humanity's sinfulness had reached a severe level, resulting in God flooding the earth and sparing only Noah, his family, and the animals on the ark. Yet the post-Flood world includes earthquakes, hurricanes, tornados, cyclones, and other natural disasters.

Does God cause every storm or tremor? Not in the way some would think. From the first hint of lightning in Noah's time, the world's weather has often followed the sinful actions of humanity. From the effects of pollution to industrial development and other human influences, many of today's climate concerns stem from our own devastating actions.

God did not originally create the world as it is today. His design was not a fallen creation, but one that was good (Genesis 1:10). Yet the impact of human life has harmed even the environment, contributing to the natural evils in our world today.

Another important aspect in this discussion is the second law of thermodynamics. This scientific law notes that the amount of unusuable energy is increasing and is irreversible. In other words, the universe is moving from order to disorder. How does this scientific concept relate to the natural evils in our world? As we know from experience, our bodies naturally decrease in strength once we pass a certain age. The same is true of our planet. What we sometimes call "acts of God" are more accurately described as acts of nature, in which the planet moves through its natural processes. The world is not perfect and is no longer even at its original stage, which God called "good" in Genesis. We live in an environment with limited, imperfect strength that sometimes reveals itself through natural disasters that harm human lives.

Isn't Religion the Source of Wars and Evil in Our World?

I've sometimes heard people claim that religion is the source of our world's wars and much evil. Even our nation's president used a recent White House prayer breakfast to remind his audience that the Crusades were the result of Christians involved in warfare, equating such activities with the violent actions of radical Islam displayed by ISIS (the Islamic State) and other terrorist groups. However, this accusation rests on a false assumption that true followers of Christ desire to perpetuate violence. True Christians do not aspire to perpetuate religion in this way, nor does the New Testament instruct Christians to do this. Christianity is about the advancement of the Gospel, the "Good News" that Jesus Christ died and rose again to pay for the sins of humanity. The Gospel is the message that each person may experience forgiveness and freedom through a personal relationship with Jesus Christ. This living relationship offered by Jesus Christ is a tangible thing—no mere ritual—and is certainly not based on meritorious efforts carried out by the believers. In reality, true followers of Jesus are as antithetical to "religion" as are skeptics.

Have religious people caused most of the wars and evil in the world? This may or may not be the case, but it would be relevant only if such people pursued war in pursuit of their religious convictions. It is clear, at least in the case of Christianity, that believers are not taught to wage war as a matter of theology. We are told, in fact, to live peaceably with everyone, if possible (Romans 12:18).

> "While other worldviews lead us to sit in the midst of life's joys, foreseeing the coming sorrows, Christianity empowers its people to sit in the midst of this world's sorrows, tasting the coming joy."
>
> Pastor/author Timothy Keller, *Walking With God Through Pain and Suffering*

Those who fail to discharge this obligation are not doing so as a result of proper religious convictions, but in spite of them. Crimes have been carried out in the name of Christianity, and this is deplorable. Regarding the rejection of Christianity in particular because of such "wars caused by religion," let's look for a moment at the evidence for the "prosecution." As far as Christianity's supposed contributions to bloodshed and suffering, the primary offense is usually said to be the Crusades, which took place during the eleventh to thirteenth centuries.

While it is true that wrongs were committed by both professed Christians and Muslims during the course of the Crusades, four things should be noted:

1. Jesus' message of salvation in no way contained an edict to kill in the name of Christianity.
2. Participants in the Crusades may or may not have been truly born-again followers of Christ. The gospel message should not be judged by the behavior of those who may have been Christians in name only.
3. The Gospel is still true regardless of failures on the part of those who may claim God's name. In other words, we are to have our eyes on Christ (who is perfect) and not on people (who are imperfect).
4. The excesses of the Crusades happened when Christians lived in violation of their Scriptures.

The Crusades in no way negate the existence of God or other essential teachings of the Christian faith. This time instead offers a vivid illustration of the evil that exists in our world and our ultimate need for Jesus Christ as the solution to sin and suffering.

The Best Hope and Power Against Suffering

How can I make the claim that Christianity offers the best hope and power against suffering? Could God have a reason for the pain we face? A look at the life of Joseph in the Bible offers much insight (Genesis 37–50). When he was seventeen, Joseph's brothers threw him into an empty well and then sold him as a slave, telling their father he was killed by a wild animal. After being sold as an Egyptian house servant, Joseph was falsely accused of attempted rape and sent to prison. In prison, he interpreted the dreams of two of Pharaoh's servants, asking them to help him secure his prison release. The one servant who returned to service forgot about Joseph for *two years*.

It was not until thirteen years after becoming a slave and then a prisoner that God provided an opportunity for Joseph to escape prison and essentially become vice president of Egypt in a single day. God used Joseph's wisdom to save the lives of many in Egypt, including his own family years later. In the end, he told his brothers, "You intended to harm me, but God intended it for good to accomplish what is now being done, the saving of many lives" (Genesis 50:20). In the New Testament, Stephen noted, "Because the patriarchs were jealous of Joseph, they sold him as a slave into Egypt. But God was with him and rescued him from all his troubles. He gave Joseph wisdom and enabled him to gain the goodwill of Pharaoh king of Egypt. So Pharaoh made him ruler over Egypt and all his palace" (Acts 7:9–10).

God can and does bring good out of evil. There is purpose in our pain. God does not allow us to suffer without reason or without hope.

"But That's Not Fair!"

Many people see the evil and suffering in our world as a string of random occurrences. They cry, "That's not fair!" when someone who is unjust experiences good things in life while the innocent appear to unfairly suffer. A look at the Old Testament often causes us to ask such questions as well. Why did God allow the Israelites to completely kill entire groups of people? How could a loving God approve of such actions? Doesn't God care about everybody?

If God were truly fair, no one would receive his goodness. Instead, God unfairly or graciously gives us many blessings, as well as the opportunity of eternal life for those who believe in Jesus Christ (1 John 5:13). If God's fairness included no mercy or grace, he would need to destroy all of us.

In addition, God certainly was not fair to many of those who followed him in the Bible. God commanded the prophet Hosea to marry an unfaithful wife. Isaiah was commanded to preach even though most would not listen to him. Jeremiah was known as the weeping prophet because he was beaten, imprisoned, and largely ignored. Jonah was commanded to preach that Nineveh would be destroyed, and then God relented from following through on his destruction.

The Old Testament book of Job presents the most detailed account of a person who faced suffering without reason. A look at this important book offers many insights into God's reasons for allowing suffering. One important aspect to note is that God can allow suffering and still care for someone. God can also work in powerful ways during and after a person suffers. When we face problems in life, it's not always because we've done something wrong. We can look back at Job's life and realize we will eventually be rewarded when we remain faithful during trials. Like Job, we can say, "I know that my redeemer lives, and in the end he will stand on the earth" (Job 19:25).

The "Violent" God of the Old Testament

But why was God so violent in the Old Testament? He allowed entire people groups to be destroyed. How is this possible?

A couple of responses can be offered. First, the Bible does not condone everything it records. Some events, such as wars, were an important part of history and were recorded as part of the story of God's people in Scripture. However, God did not approve of many of the actions recorded, especially in places like Judges 21:25, which reads, "In those days Israel had no king; everyone did as they saw fit." The book simply recorded what took place during these years, including many actions inconsistent with God's desires for his people.

However, it is true that there were a few occasions when God authorized warfare and large-scale violence. Plus, God destroyed nearly the entire human race and most animals during the time of the Flood. What was that all about? To start, in Genesis we see that with the entrance of sin into humanity, all people are deserving of death. However, God chose Abraham as the person from whom he would raise up a people to reveal his love (Genesis 12:1–3). Abraham's grandson Jacob had twelve sons who would become the twelve tribes of Israel, the nation that would receive this blessing. Yet even the Israelites were not free to live however they wished. When they sinned against God, they had to live in the desert for forty years, experienced plagues, and were taken captive as slaves to Babylon, in addition to other judgments.

> "The biblical worldview is the only one that accepts the reality of evil and suffering while giving both the cause and the purpose, while offering God-given strength and sustenance in the midst of it."
>
> Apologist Ravi Zacharias, *Jesus Among Other Gods*

It is easy to think that God may have told the Israelites to wipe out the Canaanites just because they were different or God didn't like them for some reason. But this looks at the issue from our human perspective. We see only part of the picture. God made the universe and knows how to run it better than we do. He affirms he is a good God and works toward what is ultimately good (Romans 8:28). In fact, the destruction of the Canaanites was not the annihilation of a completely innocent group of people. Their cultural practices included child sacrifice and an array of sexual immorality in addition to the worship of other gods. These were not people who simply disagreed with God on a few little details, but a people group known for violence and immorality. Plus, the Canaanites had lived this way for several hundred years, centuries during which God had given them time to change from their ways. Also, in human terms, the Israelite destruction of the Canaanites was one way of protecting themselves from future war with the Canaanites.

The "Unfair" God of the New Testament

God's "unfair" treatment of people did not end in the New Testament. John the Baptist was beheaded for serving God. Jesus was whipped, beaten, and killed by crucifixion. The disciples were arrested and beaten, and many died for their faith in Christ. The apostle Paul offered evidence of this as well. He was frequently arrested and beaten for his faith. In response, he wrote, "I will boast all the more gladly about my weaknesses, so that Christ's power may rest on me. That is why, for Christ's sake, I delight in weaknesses, in insults, in hardships, in persecutions, in difficulties. For when I am weak, then I am strong" (2 Corinthians 12:9–10).

In addition, Paul warned that God's people would face trouble. He told Timothy, "Everyone who wants to live a godly life in Christ Jesus will be persecuted" (2 Timothy 3:12). We are to expect trouble in this life. Why? We live in an imperfect world, and Christians communicate a message that not all are willing to hear.

The Christian's Suffering Is Temporary

If you've ever driven in a major city, you've probably seen a sign that says "Traffic ahead. Expect delays." In some ways, it's nice to have some kind of warning, but we are still not happy to face problems when we travel. Spiritually, we face similar frustrations in life, though the situations are often far more serious. Scripture has let us know in advance that we will face such trials, but it is still unpleasant when we do. The apostle Paul offered a helpful perspective about suffering in Romans 8:18–21:

> I consider that our present sufferings are not worth comparing with the glory that will be revealed in us. For the creation waits in eager expectation for the children of God to be revealed. For the creation was subjected to frustration, not by its own choice, but by the will of the one who subjected it, in hope that the creation itself will be liberated from its bondage to decay and brought into the freedom and glory of the children of God.

We often need to be reminded that this life is not a hundred-meter sprint but rather a marathon. Endurance during difficult times stands as an important mark of spiritual maturity. For example, 1 Peter 5:10 shares, "And the God of all grace, who called you to his eternal glory in Christ, after you have suffered a little while, will himself restore you and make you strong, firm and steadfast." Romans 5:3–4 adds, "We also glory in our sufferings, because we know that suffering produces perseverance; perseverance, character; and character, hope."

C. S. Lewis once shared, "God whispers to us in our pleasures, speaks in our conscience, but shouts in our pains: It is His megaphone to rouse a deaf world."[2] While difficult, this quotation presents an accurate way of how God works in our lives. We may not always understand the specific reasons why we face suffering or evil, but we can trust that there is a reason and that even the worst trials we face are temporary for the believer.

Myth #3

Christianity is untrue because it is based on faith instead of facts

Truth: The claims of Christianity are based on historical facts that can be tested

The family gathered for the birthday party of the oldest son. Turning twenty-five years old and celebrating a one-year anniversary since marrying his college sweetheart, Daniel was excited about his relatives coming in to join the party.

He was also looking forward to seeing his youngest brother, Clayton, a second-semester sophomore attending college in another state. Daniel had not seen Clayton since the wedding. Growing up in a Christian home, they had been very close through the years. Clayton had been a beloved youngest addition to a line of three other siblings.

Daniel had even served as a spiritual mentor to his younger brother. They grew up praying together and attending a

Christian camp together in the summer, and Daniel had attended Clayton's baptism when he made a profession of faith as a teenager.

Shortly after the blessing over the birthday meal, the conversation turned to Clayton and his studies. It turned out Clayton had been influenced by a couple of classes taught by a skeptical religious professor.

Clayton then shocked his family by announcing he was now an atheist. When his uncle began to make his best defense of God and Christianity, Clayton responded with quick answers: He believed the virgin birth of Jesus was a myth influenced by ancient paganism. The New Testament had been forged and tampered with by church leaders over the early centuries of Christianity. "And besides," Clayton argued, "No thinking person could believe in a God who would create such a violent, pain-filled, messed-up world."

The family was left in shock. Clayton's "coming out" as an atheist dampened the joy of the birthday party. The final straw was when the young man sarcastically claimed, "Don't worry, I'm still religious. I worship Richard Dawkins."

Facts, Faith, or Something Else?

This real-life account has been repeated in the lives of many young adults who have accepted the myth that Christianity is untrue because it is based on faith instead of facts. The Christian religion includes faith, but it is more than belief in the unseen. Christianity is based on historical events that can be investigated and verified.

Even those who oppose the traditionally accepted teachings of Christianity use historical information to support their case. However, the question is, Which historical information is accurate, and is this information being used accurately?

We are accustomed to seeking answers to our searches using Google or another Internet search engine that will provide us millions of hits to any keyword. The problem is not whether information exists; it's which information is best. The same can be said when investigating the key teachings of Christianity. There is much information, both biblically and historically. But which information is accurate? How is the information being used? Where does the evidence lead?

> "I am totally convinced the Christian faith is the most coherent world-view around."
>
> Ravi Zacharias, born and raised in Chennai, India, amidst a heavily Hindu culture

In this chapter, we'll look at some of the ways we can evaluate truth claims. We'll discover that the Christian faith includes many facts that can be used to support its teaching and that our study of this information can help us weigh the truth of Christianity, strengthen the faith we do have, and impact others with the message of Jesus.

Building on a Firm Foundation

Where do we begin? What facts in history support the claims of Christianity?

First, nearly all historians would agree that a man named Jesus from Nazareth was born and lived in the land of Israel two thousand years ago. He had many followers and was known for his miracles, teachings, and power over evil spirits. Jewish leaders condemned his teachings and supported his crucifixion through the Roman legal system under Pontius Pilate.[1]

Three days later, his tomb was empty. Scholar D. G. Dunn notes, "I have to say quite forcefully: the probability is that the tomb was empty. As a matter of historical reconstruction, the weight of evidence points firmly to the conclusion."[2] The alternative explanations are all worse. Many claimed to see

Jesus alive again, and the movement quickly spread. By the mid-sixties, only thirty years after Jesus, the Roman Emperor Nero blamed the fires of Rome on Christians, leading to the persecution and deaths of many early believers. Despite persecution, Christianity continued to spread, becoming the official religion of the Roman Empire in the fourth century. Even today, it is the largest single religion in the world, reaching more people in more nations than any other faith.

What is the best explanation of these historical facts? Was there a conspiracy to "invent" the resurrection account of Jesus to popularize the Christian religion? These and other allegations fail to account for the rapid growth and changed lives that have resulted from the message of Jesus. We will talk more about the details related to the resurrection later in the book, but for now I want to make it clear that the historical evidence points *toward* the faithfulness of the biblical accounts of the resurrection rather than to another explanation.

Based on Facts

Christianity is based on historical facts that can be thoroughly investigated. We have verifiable words and events, including the often bold claims of Jesus.

Christian apologetics is the field that deals with studying the facts that support the faith and responding to the questions people have about Christianity. It is based on the Greek word *apologeia,* which means to give a defense. It has nothing to do with apologizing, but rather with providing an explanation. It is the word used in 1 Peter 3:15–16: "But in your hearts revere Christ as Lord. Always be prepared to *give an answer* to everyone who asks you to give the reason for the hope that you have. But do this with gentleness and respect, keeping a clear conscience, so that those who speak maliciously against your good behavior in Christ may be ashamed of their slander."

There are several types of facts upon which Christianity is based and that apologists study. One is the trustworthiness of the Bible. Another is historical research and scientific facts that support the faith. Third, there are philosophical facts. Apologists examine and expose the logical fallacies and flawed reasoning behind popular arguments against Christianity.

Respected Christian scholars throughout history have recognized that most arguments against Christianity are based on faulty logic or inaccurate assumptions. For example, those who claim Jesus never existed defy both the early copies of the New Testament documents as well as the numerous historical writings that mention Jesus and early Christianity outside of the Bible (such as the early Jewish historian Josephus). Accusations that Christianity was built upon parallels of resurrected beings in pagan religions fail to account for the uniquenesses found in the resurrection of Jesus, the surprise of his followers, and the often backward chronology involved in these claims (that the resurrection of Jesus occurred before some of these other "resurrection" legends were popularized).

> "When we help seekers diagnose which path they're treading, assist them in avoiding its pitfalls, and expose them to the logic and evidence that uniquely support the Christian faith, we're introducing them to the only spiritual option that truly qualifies to be called the way, the truth, and the life."
>
> Lee Strobel, award-winning author, former atheist, and graduate of Yale Law School

Is There Such a Thing as Truth?

But there's no point in discussing the facts that Christianity is based on if we can't agree that facts matter and that objective truth exists.

In 1969, a group of forty Nobel Prize winners met in Stockholm, Sweden, to discuss objective meaning and morality in the modern world. The gathering was called "The place of value in a world of facts." The implication was that in a godless, purposeless, materialistic world, all that is left is just data with no real meaning.

The speakers and discussion groups concluded that humanity was headed for dark times if the modern world would continue its growing abandonment of objective truth and its foundation in God. Nobel laureate and Harvard biologist George Wald said, "The only way the world is going to stop short of the brink of nuclear holocaust is a return to God. . . . I'm convinced that this is the only way we are going to prevent the total chaos we're headed for."[3] Arthur Koestler commented on the incremental change that evolution and naturalism had brought on the culture. He faulted Darwinianism for teaching that humans are "nothing but a complex biochemical mechanism." He said, "Keep telling a man that he is nothing but an oversized rat, and he will grow whiskers and bite your fingers."[4]

School shootings, widespread violence, disregard for human life, and pervasive social unrest, all of which were at one time rare, now comprise each day's news. We may now be paying a terrible price for abandoning godly principles in many areas.

"Can there be meaning without God?" was the subject of the debate I was in a couple of years ago. During my presentations, I explained that an atheist had no objective reason for doing right. Talking with audience members afterward, one woman came up to me, clearly agitated. She handed me a business card that said "Colorado Humanist Association." She was the president.

"How dare you say that atheists can't act morally, or do good!" she exclaimed. "You don't know me; I'm an atheist but I do lots of good for others!" The lady was really angry and offended.

I'm not sure how, but she had clearly missed a significant part of my explanation about transcendent meaning and objective morality. "I didn't say atheists couldn't do good things. I was emphatic that atheists can act morally," I explained to her. "I said those who reject God don't have any objective basis for their moral actions. An atheist can do good, but his or her worldview doesn't give any absolute reason to do good."

Could God Forgive Me?

"It took me years to believe that God could even love me. It was a long time coming to accept that someone with my background could be saved."

I was speaking at a church in Paris, Tennessee. Among the people who came up to talk with me after my presentation was a man who looked as if perhaps he had seen his share of hard days. He wasn't old, probably in his late thirties or early forties. The man's face had more lines than his apparent years should have created. His jet-black hair had only a bit of gray around his temples, and it was tightly combed back. He could've easily been a walk-on in any mafia movie I've seen. Yet behind his worn face, leather jacket, and tough-guy exterior, there was a certain tenderness that seemed to emanate from him. He patiently waited in line at my book table and smiled as he approached.

"Combat left its scars on me, that's for sure," he said. "I spent years in counseling for PTSD (post-traumatic stress disorder). It was only Jesus who finally rescued me."

Rich served as a sniper for the U.S. military. Tours of duty took him through Afghanistan, Iraq, and throughout the Middle East. He explained, "Taking out any threat to American troops or civilians was my job. And I was good at it. My kill rate as a military sniper was partly due to training and partly due to the eyesight and hands God gave me, I suppose."

Speaking privately, the man told me riveting stories about his work in the Middle East. His marksmanship protected many fellow soldiers, but the hardest thing he ever had to do was take out a young mother in order to save an entire platoon. This involved shooting through a baby the woman was holding in front of her. Through the scope on his rifle, Rich could see that between her and her infant, the young woman was wearing a bomb.

For a number of agonizing seconds, his finger trembled over the trigger. Already dealing with feelings of guilt from the many kills he had performed, he put down his rifle and thought, *I can't do this, I can't do this.*

The platoon was unsuspecting as the woman silently approached. Looking again through his scope, he saw the woman begin to reach and motion in a way that he knew would trigger some sort of detonator. From where he was, the infant she was carrying blocked her body. Having no other recourse, and knowing that the lives of a platoon were at stake, he fired. Only seconds before what would have been disastrous, the woman—and the infant strapped to her chest—lay dead.

"How could God love me after all the killing I had done? Doesn't his Word say, 'Thou shalt not kill'? I contemplated suicide, thinking I could just get the inevitable over with."

The man's story was hard to hear. But joy was clearly evident on his face as he said, "I can honestly say that Jesus not only saves, he heals. He saved my soul and healed my emotions. Each day is a journey, and very often a struggle. But Jesus does forgive, and he restores."

Forgiveness is an important aspect of the Christian faith. Many people reject Christianity because they feel God could never forgive them. Yet God promises to forgive anyone who trusts in him (1 John 1:9). It is not a matter of being good enough for God to forgive us; he offers forgiveness regardless of our actions. This is something God states as a fact, and those who receive often experience emotionally. Facts are the basis for the faith we have in Jesus, but these are not cold, hard facts that have no impact. These truths still transform lives today.

What About You?

Christianity is based on facts that lead to faith. Maybe one of those people new to the realms of doubt and unbelief is you. Perhaps you have questions about God that have remained unanswerable. Maybe you were raised in a Christian home, attended Christian school, but now the simple trust in Jesus you experienced as a child seems impossible to maintain.

Let me encourage you not to give up. Seek the truth. Maybe the barrier keeping you from truly living for God is taking the time to investigate some of the difficulties you see in Christianity. Whether your concern is God's existence, the resurrection, or the problem of evil in our world, keep seeking. Jesus said, "Ask and it will be given to you; seek and you will find; knock and the door will be opened to you. For everyone who asks receives; the one who seeks finds; and to the one who knocks, the door will be opened" (Matthew 7:7–8). God says, "You will seek me and find me when you seek me with all your heart" (Jeremiah 29:13).

> "I am an historian, I am not a believer, but I must confess as an historian that this penniless preacher from Nazareth is irrevocably the very center of history. Jesus Christ is easily the most dominant figure in all history."
>
> H. G. Wells

Myth #4

Christianity has been disproven by modern science

Truth: The latest scientific evidence points to an Intelligent Designer behind all creation

The popular film *God's Not Dead* portrays Christian college student Josh Wheaton attending a philosophy class with an avowed atheist instructor named Professor Radisson. When the professor instructs his students to write the words "God is dead" on the first day of class, Josh refuses. Instead, Josh is required to present the evidence for his views throughout the class, culminating in a debate with his professor to end the semester.

One of the professor's objections to the Christian faith is that it conflicts with science. Science presents a worldview that both does not require God and reveals no need for God. If Darwin was right and all forms of life evolved from one another, then how can the biblical account of creation in six days be true? Christianity appears to be disproven by modern science.

But this isn't quite the full story. Over the past generation of scientific scholarship, a new wave of data increasingly points toward a different conclusion. While skeptical scientists still refuse to claim God is behind creation, a fresh movement has arisen that scientifically supports the Christian worldview of the universe's origin. What is it? The Intelligent Design movement.

What Is Intelligent Design and Why Does It Matter?

Intelligent Design (sometimes called design theory or ID) is a position regarding life's origins. To be clear, ID is not a direct argument for the Bible or for the gospel of Jesus Christ. Educator and author William Dembski said, "This is a very modest, minimalist position. It doesn't speculate about a creator or his intentions."[1] But Intelligent Design is a view that is *consistent* with a biblical worldview.

What is Intelligent Design? Simply put, this view states that the structure of information found in the natural world points toward a powerful and intelligent outside source of origin. In other words, the universe is neither eternal, nor did it create itself. Intelligent Design says that the best explanation for the origin of the universe is a powerful and wise external source of all space, time, energy, and matter.

> "The more we get to know about our universe, the more the hypothesis that there is a Creator . . . gains in credibility as the best explanation of why we are here."
>
> Oxford professor
> John Lennox, PhD

Evidence supporting this view has arisen from both extremes of the natural realm. On one side, the study of astronomy has observed the farthest reaches of the galaxy in a search for clues regarding the universe's origin. Claiming to reach back to nearly the point following the Big Bang, astronomers note clearly a point of origin for all space, time, energy, and matter. A variety of lines of evidence have been collected since the launch of the Hubble telescope that have led to a new consensus among astronomers that our universe had a singular point of origin that required a powerful outside source of creation.

On the other end of the spectrum, researchers of molecular biology have unearthed new details that far transcend what was available during the life of Charles Darwin. Instead of discovering new information that supports evolutionary biology, researchers are finding complex information that points toward a source beyond the known world. Dr. Stephen C. Meyer, who holds a PhD in the Philosophy of Science from Cambridge, notes in the introduction of his groundbreaking book *Signature of the Cell*:

> In his theory of evolution, Charles Darwin never sought to unravel the mystery of where biological information comes from. For him, the origins of life remained shrouded in impenetrable obscurity. While the digital code in DNA first came to light in the 1950s, it wasn't until later that scientists began to sense the implications behind the exquisitely complex technical system for processing and storing information in the cell. The cell does what any advanced computer operating system can do but with almost inconceivably greater suppleness and efficiency.[2]

Now wrap your mind around this: An individual human cell consists of an estimated 10 to 100 trillion atoms. It possesses and manages more information than a full set of encyclopedias. Scientists still disagree on the number of cells that make up the entire human body, but the numbers are in the trillions. And each cell in your body has a copy of your own DNA—an information "recipe" for you—encoded, arranged, and stored by means of four characters.

If, while walking on the beach, we found "Bob loves Julie" written in the sand, we would rightly assume that something more than just the motion of the waves was responsible. Living things contain information much more complex than that, but the point is clear: This universe of complicated things bears undeniable evidence of having been intentionally created.

Meyer's next book, *Darwin's Doubt*, dealt with Darwin's nagging concern regarding the missing finds in the fossil record. Darwin's theory required that future discoveries would show that the record of animal life would reveal a progressive chain from less complex to more complex forms of life. However, findings since Darwin's time have caused concern regarding this view. Instead, the Cambrian Explosion shows an array of animal life appearing in the same time period without precursors (previous, less complex predecessors). Again, the evidence increasingly points toward a view of complex life appearing at once, just as is seen in the biblical account of creation.

> "There is enough information capacity in a single human cell to store the *Encyclopedia Britannica*, all 30 volumes of it, three or four times over."
>
> Atheist Richard Dawkins

The First Cause

Ancient philosophy has also long addressed the beginning of the universe. Aristotle was the philosopher known for coining the idea of the First Cause, or an Unmoved Mover, who is the beginning of all things. Dr. William Lane Craig popularized the particular form of the cosmological argument called the Kalam argument.[3] It states,

- The universe began to exist.
- Whatever begins to exist has a cause for its existence.
- Therefore, the universe has a cause for its existence.

In defense of the first premise, both scientific and philosophical evidence point to the fact that the universe began to exist a finite time ago. Scientific evidence for the beginning of the universe includes the expanding universe and the second law of thermodynamics. The philosophical evidence for the beginning of the universe includes the impossibility of traversing an actual infinite length of time and the impossibility of the past being infinite, because of the impossibility of traversing an actual infinite length of time. In maintaining the evidence for the expanding universe, scientists maintain that every object in the universe is moving away from every other object. Thus, space itself is expanding. Physicist George Gamow says, "The entire space of the universe, populated by billions of galaxies, is in a state of rapid expansion, with its members flying away from one another at high speed."[4]

> "A commonsense interpretation of the facts suggests that a superintellect has monkeyed with physics. . . . The numbers one calculates from the facts seem to me so overwhelming as to put this conclusion almost beyond question."
>
> Fred Hoyle (1915–2001), astronomer who coined the term *Big Bang*

My friends Dr. Norman Geisler and Jason Jimenez also note:

> According to Gottfried Wilhelm Leibniz (1646–1716), a German philosopher and mathematician, everything that exists has a cause for its existence. We know the universe exists and didn't get here on its own. God is the necessary being who produces external causes that don't exist necessarily because they are contingent on something greater than their own existence.
>
> But there are two other options: (1) *Naturalism* teaches that nothing created the universe—it just came to be with no real explanation. (2) *Pantheism* teaches that God and the universe are one and eternally the same. The problem with naturalism is that it holds to a contradictory claim that *nothing created something or something created itself*. But this is fundamentally irrational. Pantheism, on the other hand,

is fundamentally flawed because it identifies the universe as eternal, when the Second Law of Thermodynamics proves that wrong.

Thus, it is reasonable to conclude that God created the universe out of nothing (*ex nihilo*).[5]

Theism, or belief in an all-powerful, Intelligent Designer behind all of creation, is not only a reasonable conclusion, but the best conclusion based on the evidence.

Scripture's Record of Nature

Interestingly, this is what the first ten words of the Bible reveal: "In the beginning God created the heavens and the earth" (Genesis 1:1). While all Bible-believing Christians would agree with this first verse, the agreement often ends beyond this point.

> "Many investigators feel uneasy about stating in public that the origin of life is a mystery, even though behind closed doors they freely admit they are baffled."
>
> Paul Davies, PhD, renowned physicist; director of SETI project

A wide variety of thoughts and opinions exist regarding *how* God created and designed the universe, but both science and Scripture agree on a starting point—an outside, Intelligent Designer who made all things.

Maybe you are one of those people who grew up in a church or Christian home who had doubts about the relationship between science and Scripture. When you asked questions, maybe your parents or even your minister belittled your curiosity and made you feel dumb for even asking tough questions about the creation's origin. Let me encourage you—your questions are perfectly acceptable to God. He created the world and has revealed much through both his book of nature and his book of Scripture. Properly understood, science and Scripture do not contradict each other; they complement each other.

But what about the length of creation? Adam and Eve? The animals on Noah's ark? Scripture reveals some of the story, but not all. Science answers details in other areas, but not every detail. Instead, let me share some lines of agreement where we can find consistency between the scientific evidence and God's revelation that can strengthen our faith in him.

God Is the Intelligent Designer

Christians look at the evidence from science and conclude God is the Intelligent Designer behind all forms of life. Some may disagree with this particular view of the Intelligent Designer, but the facts are consistent with an all-powerful, wise, and caring God behind the universe. As Psalm 19:1–4 declares:

> The heavens declare the glory of God;
>   the skies proclaim the work of his hands.
> Day after day they pour forth speech;
>   night after night they reveal knowledge.
> They have no speech, they use no words;
>   no sound is heard from them.
> Yet their voice goes out into all the earth,
>   their words to the ends of the world.

God Created the Planets, Moons, and Stars

There are two main biblical views regarding God's creation of the universe. One view holds that God created all of the planets, moons, and stars in Genesis 1:1 when he created the heavens and the earth, later revealing aspects like the sun and moon by making them "appear" from the perspective of someone on the earth. A second interpretation states that God physically made the sun, moon, and stars on day four. Either way, God is the Creator and provided these elements for the benefit of those on the earth.

It amazes me that God placed this little blue speck far enough away from the sun that life could be sustained without melting, yet close enough that all forms of life would not freeze to death. Even a short distance one way or the other would end all life on earth as we know it. God placed this planet and the elements that surround it in perfect harmony to support his activities on the earth—including your life and mine.

God Directly Created All Forms of Life

As we've discussed, the latest scientific evidence points toward an outside, direct source for the creation of all forms of life. This would exclude evolution from one form of life to another. In other words, a fish did not evolve into an amphibian, then into a monkey, and ultimately into a human. Each "kind" of life-form began in a particular, complex way.

This also finds its basis in the biblical account of creation. Many Christians will dispute the length of the "days" of creation, but the account is clear that God created plant life, all forms of animal life, and human life. God created vegetation on the third day (Genesis 1:12–13), animal life on days five and six (Genesis 1:20–24), and human life on day six (Genesis 1:26–27).

What about evolution? There are two ways evolution is discussed—macroevolution and microevolution. Macroevolution is the theory that one kind or type of life-form can evolve into another. This is the type of evolution Darwin proposed took place in the earth's early history. To be clear, this type of evolution is a theory, not a fact. Macroevolution has never been witnessed or re-created in a lab.

The second type of evolution is microevolution. This is the term used to explain the various species of dogs, for example. All species of dogs are still dogs, but breeding and genetics can cause variation from one species of dog to another.

A German shepherd and Labrador retriever are, ultimately, both still dogs.

Both science and the Bible can be used to reject macroevolution. Unless someone could naturally observe macroevolution in nature, it will only remain a theory. Even if scientists could "evolve" one type of animal into another in a lab, it would be with outside, informed assistance rather than natural processes. Microevolution, however, is an observable phenomenon that should be of no concern to Christians.

> "Darwinism is not a testable scientific theory, but a *metaphysical research program.*"
>
> Karl Popper (1902–1994), philosopher of science

Skeptics have long wondered why Christians are so resistant to science, specifically evolution. Isn't it possible that the Bible alludes to evolution as being the tool God used in creating the world? Genesis 2:7 says, "The Lord God formed a man from the dust of the ground and breathed into his nostrils the breath of life, and the man became a living being."

This discussion must take into account the reality that evolution and revelation have vastly different things to say about the subject of origins. As Darwinian evolutionists have long pointed out, a naturalistic model of understanding the universe is inherently nontheistic (that is, no Creator is present nor necessary).

Shortly after the famous Scopes trial in Dayton, Tennessee, which brought the conflict between creation and evolution to a national focus, the president of the American Association for the Advancement of Atheism wrote, "Evolution is atheism." In his book *River Out of Eden: A Darwinian View of Life*, Richard Dawkins famously summarized the evolutionist's assumptions about the forces at work in this world: "At bottom, no design, no purpose, no evil and no good, nothing but blind, pitiless indifference."[6]

Statements like this illustrate the traditionally impassable gulf that separates these two views. Those on both sides of the issue have noted that "theistic evolution" (belief that God used evolution as his tool for creation) is tough to defend. Each position includes core assumptions that conflict with the other. If the core beliefs of each side are upheld consistently, the believer in evolution and the believer in creation will inevitably reach an impasse.

The incompatibility of the two models is illustrated in the asking of only three basic questions. These are the questions of origin, purpose, and destiny. People throughout history have pondered core questions like these:

- Where did everything—including me—originate?
- Why am I here? What is life's meaning?
- Where is the world headed? What happens after death?

In response to such pervasive, big questions, a non-theistic worldview provides answers that are inherently naturalistic. A theistic worldview gives responses that are inherently supernatural. Again, if the core assumptions of the worldviews are handled consistently, any attempted integration of the two carries with it potential for conflict.

The challenging issues in such a discussion yield problematic answers. Think about the Judeo-Christian view of what it means to be human. If the image of God in humanity came about miraculously, why not accept that God miraculously brought about physical life in forming man from the dust of the earth? If God could be solely responsible for the spiritual part of man's nature, why not attribute to him the physical?

God Created the First People

A relatively recent idea suggests that Adam and Eve were not the first people but rather were merely representations of the first humans. For secular scientists or sociologists, this may not be of much importance. However, Jesus personally referred to Adam and Eve as the first humans (Matthew 19:4–5). The apostle Paul also referred to Adam as the first man (Romans 5:12–14) and to Eve as the first woman (1 Timothy 2:13).

What about the origin of Adam's wife, Eve? The Bible says that God put Adam in a state of deep sleep, took from his side a rib, and from this made the first woman (Genesis 2). I think two things are worth noting: first, that the apostle Paul referred to Eve as a literal, historical person (1 Timothy 2:13); and further, that discoveries within a number of scientific disciplines (genetics, biochemistry, and geology, to name a few) indicate that the human race originated from a single male-female pair.

Chemist Fazale Rana, PhD, and astrophysicist Hugh Ross, PhD, discuss this at length in their book *Who Was Adam?* Rana and Ross state:

> Genetic studies of human population groups signify that humanity had a recent origin in a single geographical location from a small population, with genetic links back to a single man and single woman. . . . In fact, the first genetic ancestors of humanity are referred to in the scientific community as Y-chromosomal Adam and mitochondrial Eve.[7]

The Bible frequently mentions Adam and Eve as the first people on the planet. Though there will probably be more findings that suggest the first humans were "discovered" in some other location than the biblical Garden of Eden, there is no clear evidence that contradicts the possibility of Adam and Eve as the first people God made. Instead, science increasingly supports the view that the first humans required an outside creator. While odd views, including the possibility of aliens, have been suggested, there is no reason the first two humans could not have been created just as Genesis explains.

Elsewhere Scripture affirms God's hand in creation as well. Paul and Barnabas told their audience at Lystra, "We too are only human, like you. We are bringing you good news, telling you to turn from these worthless things to the living God, who made the heavens and the earth and the sea and everything in them" (Acts 14:15). Paul wrote to the Romans, "For since the creation of the world God's invisible qualities—his eternal power and divine nature—have been clearly seen" (Romans 1:20). The biblical information can be found far beyond Genesis. The Old and New Testaments repeatedly affirm God as the Creator of all things.

What About the Age of the Universe?

In the now famous Bill Nye–Ken Ham debate on creation, a large portion of the discussion focused on the age of the universe. While postulations about the age of the earth make for interesting discussion among both Christians and non-Christians, let me say two important things: First, no one knows for sure the exact age of the universe. They just don't. Second, the Christian message is more about the destiny of your soul (which we can be sure of), rather than the age of the planet (which is open to question).

I am not saying that the age of the universe isn't an important topic. If you take Scripture to be accurate (that is, *true*) and authoritative (that is, *relevant to the lives of all people*), then what God's Word says about creation is obviously important. Personally, passages in Genesis and elsewhere lead me to conclude that there were six literal, twenty-four-hour days in which God created all things. Even my friend William Dembski, PhD (a Christian colleague who holds to an "old earth" position), has said that a plain reading of the Bible is more likely to lead one to a "young earth" position than to an "old earth" position.[8]

But questions about the age of the universe should not in any way prevent people from reaching positive conclusions about Jesus Christ, who gave his life for the forgiveness of our sins! Impassioned arguments are made by all, regardless of beliefs about origins. However, entering into a relationship with God really has nothing to do with what one believes about how old the universe is. A definitive number on the earth's age, I suspect, we will never know. But the age of the universe is less important than the reality of the Creator of the universe. If we can find reasonable evidence that God created all things, including all forms of life, then the time taken to do so is of secondary importance.

The concern for those who accept the Bible as authoritative is primarily related to the definition of the six "days" of creation in Genesis 1 and 2. Did God intend for readers to understand these periods as twenty-four-hour blocks of time or not?

Let's lay down a few lines of discussion: First, it is true that the Hebrew word used for "day" can refer to more than just a twenty-four-hour day. It can also refer to day as in "daytime," day as in "the time of," or "part of a day." In other words, either view can be considered a "literal" view.

Second, one's understanding of the days of Genesis is separate from one's understanding of evolution. In other words, someone who believes Genesis refers to long periods of time can also reject Darwinian evolution, just as a young earth Creationist does.

Third, there is controversy regarding these two views because there are some details that are not easy to understand. For example, how could twenty-four-hour days exist prior to the fourth day and the creation of the sun and moon? This question is not one associated with modern evolution but rather was expressed by the theologian Augustine more than fifteen hundred years ago. He noted that, at the very least, Christians should be open to the possibility of unknown periods of time prior to day four of creation.

Others have offered questions about day six of creation. Adam seems to have accomplished a lot of work for one day. He named all of the animals in one day, could not find a helper suitable for himself, took a nap, Eve was created, and they were married. He was a busy guy! While it's possible all of these events took place in one day, it is easy to understand why some would express questions about all of these activities happening in one twenty-four-hour time period.

The core truths to glean from God's creation include that he is the Intelligent Designer, the Creator of the universe, and the direct Creator of all forms of life. While there may be room for discussion regarding some areas of God's creative process, the Bible's essential message is consistent with the scientific evidence found in our world today.

Shouldn't we expect that the One who made the heavens and the earth would be accurate in his reporting of his creation? While we are limited and finite in our understanding of God's amazing ability to design the universe around us, we can certainly seek to observe his hand at work and worship him in response.

Regarding the impact of Intelligent Design on faith, Meyer notes:

> Of course, many continue to dismiss intelligent design as nothing but "religion masquerading as science." They point to the theory's obviously friendly implications for theistic belief as a justification for classifying and dismissing the theory as "religion." But such critics confuse the implications of the theory of intelligent design with its evidential basis. The theory of intelligent design may well have theistic implications. But that is not grounds for dismissing it. Scientific theories must be judged by their ability to explain evidence, not by whether they have

undesirable implications. Those who say otherwise flout logic and overlook the clear testimony of the history of science.[9]

That "God is not dead" is clear to anyone who looks up at the stars at night. Science does not disprove God's existence. Science helps us to discover the intricate details involved in God's design of the world around us. Only a God who loves us and cares about the universe in which we live would work to such lengths to provide for the needs of our world and our lives.

Myth #5

Christianity is not a religion for the educated

Truth: Many of the world's top past and present scholars are Christians

A startling study observed that "religious people are less intelligent than non-believers."[1] Is this true? Has it been proven that Christianity is not a religion for the educated?

This appears to be the message popular culture presents today. The idea that the term *Christian* could be consistent with an educated, intelligent person is seen as inconsistent and illogical. However, those who communicate this message offer only one side of the story. In my graduate studies, I vividly remember the first week of my course in church history. Part of me dreaded the idea of reading lists of names and events from the centuries, thinking back to my days of goofing off in high school history. But the history of the church involved a much different emphasis than any course on the history of nations or wars. Rather than discovering uninteresting trivia of people long forgotten, I was awakened to a diverse world of Christians, including many of the world's top scholars, who have embraced the message of Jesus and seen it consistent with other areas of learning.

In this chapter, I want to share some of these stories with you. Why? Not to simply inform, but rather to inspire. Many men and women throughout the past two thousand years have found the Christian worldview the most consistent and persuasive way of life, committing themselves to its study and application. From the apostle Paul to the intellectuals of the twenty-first century, you'll find a network of bright minds who demonstrate that Christianity is the belief system of some of the most educated people throughout history.

New Testament Intellectuals

The origin of Christianity is recorded in the New Testament, making it the best place to begin our journey. Though the apostles originally consisted of mostly fishermen, there was one tax collector, Matthew, who has left us with a gospel that displays his wisdom and literary ability. The apostle John also left a gospel, along with three letters (1–3 John) and the book of Revelation. The gospel of Mark is traditionally believed to be the recorded teachings of the apostle Peter, while Luke, an associate of the apostle Paul, was a medical doctor turned missionary who left two of the largest and most literary writings of the New Testament (Luke and Acts).

> "The Christian faith does not call for us to put our minds on the shelf, to fly in the face of common sense and history, or to make a leap of faith into the dark. The rational person, fully apprised of the evidence, can confidently believe . . ."
>
> Philosopher William Lane Craig, PhD

Yet it is the apostle Paul who is noted as the primary intellectual of the New Testament period. Trained as a Jewish scholar under the renowned Gamaliel, Paul held the equivalent of a doctoral degree in religion. After his radical transformation as a follower of Christ (Acts 9), he used his abilities to pen thirteen of the New Testament's writings. Among these is the letter to the Romans, considered the most advanced theological work of the early church.

The Early Church

The next generations of the Christian movement included the first speakers and writers who presented evidence to support the Christian faith using the methods of argument popular in their time. Many of these writings can be found in the works of the Ante-Nicene Fathers, including Justin Martyr, Tatian, Irenaeus, and Polycarp.

Justin Martyr, considered one of the first Christian apologists (early second century), used philosophy and Scripture to defend against early false teachings in the church and society. Many of his works have been lost, but his *First Apology* was addressed to Emperor Antoninus Pius to defend religious freedom for Christians and explain the basis for Christian practices. It provided a Christian worldview that serves as the basis for many works by those who defend the faith today.

Irenaeus (died c. 202) also served as an early apologist and theologian. His best-known work, *Against Heresies*, provided a response to early Gnostic teachings, emphasizing the writings of the New Testament and the traditions of the early church as authoritative. He also served as one of the first writers to note the four gospels as canonical or authoritative in the churches.

One of the great voices of the early church period was the man known as St. Augustine. There were several significant rational turning points in Augustine's life before he came to Christ. Augustine reasoned his way out of total skepticism by seeing the self-defeating nature of it. He studied another writer named Plotinus. Augustine informs us that he would not even have been able to conceive of a spiritual being, let alone believe in one, without further study. His works, including *The City of God*, have influenced the church and Western culture in profound ways.

In the late fourth century, the church father Jerome provided a monumental service to the church when he directed the efforts to translate the Hebrew and Greek Scriptures into what became known as the Latin Vulgate. His influence in languages and literature helped provide a translation of Scripture used throughout Western churches for the next one thousand years.

St. Thomas Aquinas (1225–1274) also stands out among the leaders of church history. Serving as a Catholic priest in the thirteenth century, he developed philosophical works, including arguments for the existence of God, which became the standard in philosophy for his generation and beyond. His best-known work, the *Summa Theologica*, was originally 3,500 pages of philosophy and theology that marked these fields as important intellectual pursuits.

In 1517, a German monk named Martin Luther nailed his Ninety-five Theses to the door of the church in Wittenberg, protesting the excesses of Roman Catholic traditions and practices. His efforts became known as the start of the Protestant Reformation, focusing on the Bible as the sole authority for the church, and salvation by faith in Christ alone. In addition, he helped translate the Bible into the German language, contributing greatly to both cultural and spiritual change in Germany and throughout Europe.

John Calvin (1509–1564), a French theologian during the Reformation, completed the first edition of *The Institutes of the Christian Religion* while he was in his twenties. His written works have endured as some of the most popular in European history, developing early Protestant theology into a powerful force.

Modern Intellectuals Who Believed

These accounts are helpful to better understand the involvement of certain intellectuals in the early centuries of the church, but what about today? Do those who objectively analyze the Christian faith still come to the conclusion that it is true?

You may have seen **J. Warner Wallace** on TV programs dealing with unsolved crimes. Warner, who spent two decades as a cold-case homicide detective, began as an outspoken atheist. After years of opposing Christianity, at thirty-five years old, Warner "took a serious and expansive look at the evidence for the Christian worldview and determined that Christianity was demonstrably true."[2] His book *Cold-Case Christianity* chronicles aspects of cold-case investigations as applied to the reliability of the gospel accounts. His efforts have been highlighted on many major media programs including NBC's *Dateline*, Fox News, and Court TV.

Frank Morison was a skeptical attorney who set out to disprove Christianity by showing that the resurrection never took place. His quest ended with his conversion and a book titled *Who Moved the Stone?* in which the first chapter was titled "The Book that Refused to Be Written." His well-researched conclusion was that the most likely explanation for the empty tomb was the resurrection of Jesus. The final words of his popular book declared, "There may be, and, as the writer thinks, there certainly is, a deep and profoundly historical basis for that much disputed sentence in the Apostles' Creed—'The third day he rose again from the dead.'"[3] He became a Christian and influenced many other intellectuals to consider the claims of Christianity.

In the early twentieth century, Harvard professor of law **Simon Greenleaf**, who had written a book on legal evidence, was challenged by students to apply the rules of legal evidence to the New Testament to see if its testimony would stand up in court. The result was a book titled *The Testimony of the Evangelists*, in which he expresses his confidence in the basic documents and truths of the Christian faith.

Cambridge scholar **C. S. Lewis**, a former atheist perhaps best known as author of the *Chronicles of Narnia* series, was converted to Christianity on the basis of the evidence, according to his biographical work *Surprised by Joy*. He recalls, "I thought I had the Christians 'placed' and disposed of forever." But, "A young man who wishes to remain a sound atheist cannot be too careful of his reading. There are traps everywhere—'Bibles laid open, millions of surprises,' as Herbert says, 'Fine nets and stratagems.' God is, if I may say it, very unscrupulous."[4]

But C. S. Lewis became a Christian because, to him, the evidence was compelling and he could not escape it. Lewis referred to himself as the most reluctant convert in Britain: He was "brought in kicking, struggling, resentful, and darting [my] eyes in every direction for a chance of escape." The God "whom I so earnestly desired not to meet" became his Lord and Savior.[5] His book on Christian evidences, *Mere Christianity*, is considered a classic and has been responsible for persuading countless numbers of people regarding the Gospel.

As a pre-law student, **Josh McDowell** was also a skeptic of Christianity. No Christians McDowell had encountered to that point in his life seemed credible, and the message they believed appeared to him equally vacuous. However, some Christian friends during his college years eventually prodded McDowell into taking a serious look at the Bible and Jesus. He surprisingly found himself engrossed in the investigation, and states, "As a result, I found historical facts and evidence about Jesus Christ that I never knew existed."[6] He eventually wrote a number of important texts in defense of Christianity, among them *Evidence That Demands a Verdict* and the bestselling *More Than a Carpenter.*

Though raised a Christian, **Gary Habermas**, PhD, went through a season in which he rejected his previous faith. Questioning Christianity, Habermas experienced doubts about God and the Bible, and for a time gave serious consideration to Buddhism. He concluded that while the resurrection could be believed, he was personally skeptical that any evidence for it was convincing. However, after closer examination, the evidence brought him around and he concluded the resurrection was an established fact of history. He has since become known as the world's top expert on research related to the resurrection of Jesus Christ and has authored numerous books on the topic.

As a philosophy student at Cornell University, **John Warwick Montgomery** was a convinced skeptic. After being challenged to investigate the evidence for Christianity, he soon converted. He recalls, "I went to the university as a 'garden-variety' twentieth-century pagan. And as a result of being forced, for intellectual integrity's sake, to check out this evidence, I finally came around."[7] He confessed that had it not been for a committed undergraduate student who continued to challenge him to really examine the evidence, he would never have believed.[8]

Montgomery graduated from Cornell University with distinction in philosophy. He earned a PhD from the University of Chicago, a second doctorate in theology from the University of Strasbourg, France, plus seven additional graduate degrees in theology, law, library science, and other fields. He has written over 125 scholarly journal articles and forty books.

Well-known author **Malcolm Muggeridge** was also once a skeptic of Christianity. Near the end of his life he became fully convinced of the truth of the resurrection of Jesus, writing a book entitled *Jesus: The Man Who Lives* (1975). He wrote, "The coming of Jesus into the world is the most stupendous event in human history. . . ." and "What is unique about Jesus is that, on the testimony and in the experience of innumerable people, of all sorts and conditions, of all races and nationalities from the simplest and most primitive to the most sophisticated and cultivated, he remains alive. . . . Either Jesus never was or he still is. . . . With the utmost certainty, I assert he still is."[9]

Archaeologist and Oxford professor **Sir William Ramsay** was once a skeptic of Christianity, convinced that the Bible was fraudulent. "He had spent years deliberately preparing himself for the announced task of heading an exploration expedition into Asia Minor and Palestine, the home of the Bible, where he would 'dig up the evidence' that the Bible was the product of ambitious monks. . . . He regarded the weakest spot in the whole New Testament to be the story of Paul's travels. These had never been thoroughly investigated [at that time]. He spent fifteen years literally 'digging for the evidence.' Then in 1896 he published a large volume, *Saint Paul the Traveler and the Roman Citizen*," which instead showed that the evidence supported the writings of the New Testament.[10]

Former *Chicago Tribune* law reporter **Lee Strobel** was a devout atheist until his wife came home and shared she had become a Christian. He began to attend church services and research the New Testament in an effort to convince her that Christianity was not true. By the end of two years, his studies led him to the belief that Jesus did indeed resurrect from the dead and is the Son of God. His popular book *The Case for Christ* chronicles this story along with his interviews of top scholars in this process.

Why Christianity Can Stand the Evidence of Intellectual Research

People send me pictures. Lots of pictures. Some photos they take with their mobile devices, and other times they are pictures they find online. Pictures of what, you ask? Oftentimes, topics I reference in my speaking prompt people to email items in. Sometimes the pictures/news stories/anecdotes are funny, sometimes poignant. Nearly always thought-provoking.

Recently I received a photo of a church marquee that read, "Reason Is the Greatest Enemy That Faith Has." Two hours after this hit my inbox, the photo was in my video presentation for the evening. When this slide came up, I asked the audience, "Do you agree with this church's sign? Why or why not?"

To my surprise, more than one-third expressed agreement that reason is the greatest enemy of faith. Thus began an engaging discussion with members of the audience. I pointed out (and it should also be noted here) that believers, seekers, and active non-believers all approach the issue of faith with certain presuppositions in their minds. Not one of us is truly a blank slate with no ideas/biases/facts/distortions in our minds. We all have preconceived assumptions we carry around in our heads that may or may not be correct—even the atheist's conviction that he is blissfully objective and unbiased when it comes to issues of faith.

Not only is reason not the enemy of faith, but the fact is that no thought is possible without logic and rationality. The question is not, Should I engage in reason? The questions we must hold before ourselves are, Am I reasoning well? Am I reaching valid conclusions?

Some eight hundred years ago, St. Thomas Aquinas taught that every possible argument against Christianity has a rational mistake in it somewhere.[11] I agree. Aquinas was a great defender of the faith, likely one of the most intelligent persons

> "If there be any difficulties in the faith of Christ, they are not one-tenth as great as the absurdities in any system of unbelief which seeks to take its place."
>
> Charles Spurgeon
> (1834–1892)

who ever lived, and not inconsequentially, his scholarship and life contributed to Europe *not* becoming Muslim during the Middle Ages. I think that Aquinas would be sad today to know that much of the world is unaware of the rational evidence strongly supporting Christianity. Even some in the church (in the West, at least) seem to pride themselves on ignoring reason. Logic, a reasoned defense of the faith, and careful scholarship are sometimes dismissed as being "the wisdom of men" (1 Corinthians 2:5 NKJV).

How Did Christianity Get Its Bad Reputation?

It is little wonder that Christianity is assumed by some to be the stock and trade of uneducated people. Logical proofs exist, yet Christianity has gained a reputation for not being an intellectually honest or compelling faith. Let's take a look at some of the "uneducated" attitudes toward Christianity and then talk about why it is important to discuss faith in an intellectually intelligent manner.

"The Bible Doesn't Need to Be Defended"

One of the reasons Christianity has gained a reputation as an uneducated religion is found in the attitude of some Christians that states, "The Bible doesn't need to be defended." Hebrews 4:12 is often cited, noting, "For the word of God is alive and active. Sharper than any double-edged sword, it penetrates even to dividing soul and spirit, joints and marrow; it judges the thoughts and attitudes of the heart." While God's Word is powerful, this does not negate the need for Christians to present the evidence that supports faith.

90

If someone from another religion wanted to convert you to his or her religion, would you be satisfied if he or she simply said, "My religion's book is powerful. I do not need to defend it. Just read it and you will be convinced"? We would not likely find this claim compelling, would we? Why not? We would want some evidence.

"Only Faith Can Please God"

Others have taken the approach that only faith can please God, so why bother with convincing someone with evidence? This is based on Hebrews 11:6, "Without faith it is impossible to please God." These Christians appeal only to the emotional, feeling side of Christianity in sharing their faith with others. Yet Jesus made an important claim in answering the question, "What is the greatest commandment?" He answered, "Love the Lord your God with all your heart and with all your soul and with *all your mind*. This is the first and greatest commandment" (Matthew 22:37–38, emphasis added).

What does it mean to love the Lord with all of our mind? This would certainly include learning what the Bible teaches, the evidence that supports it, and how to communicate this information to others. In fact, this type of learning and sharing is essential in discussing faith with those who rely heavily on intellectual reasons in making decisions. Again, as 1 Peter 3:15 teaches, "Always be prepared to give an answer."

"Only God Can Change the Heart"

I've heard many well-meaning Christians over the years say, "Only God can change the heart." While this is true, those who use this phrase often mean they will not try to convince unbelievers that Christ is Lord. Instead, they intend to only pray for them or show kindness and "leave the rest" to God.

While both prayer and showing compassion to unbelievers are essential parts of sharing our faith, they are only *part*. At some point, a person will have questions about the information presented in the Bible, whether Jesus really did return to life, or how the universe began. To rely on the response "Only God can change the heart" will leave many important questions unanswered for those seeking truth.

Why Do Christians Feel the Need to Defend Their Faith?

There are several important reasons to provide answers to the questions people have regarding the Christian faith. God commands it, people need it, and the changed lives of many former skeptics confirm it.

First, God commands Christians to answer the questions others have about faith. In addition to Peter's words in 1 Peter 3:15–16, six other places in Scripture emphasize the importance of providing answers to others. (Italicized words note the use of the Greek word *apologeia*.)

- Acts 22:1: "Brothers and fathers, listen now to my *defense*."
- Acts 25:16: "I told them that it is not the Roman custom to hand over anyone before they have faced their accusers and have had an opportunity to *defend* themselves against the charges."
- 1 Corinthians 9:3: "This is my *defense* to those who sit in judgment on me."
- 2 Corinthians 7:11: "See what this godly sorrow has produced in you: what earnestness, what eagerness to *clear yourselves*, what indignation, what alarm, what longing, what concern, what readiness to see justice done. At every point you have proved yourselves to be innocent in this matter."

- Philippians 1:7: "It is right for me to feel this way about all of you, since I have you in my heart and, whether I am in chains or *defending* and confirming the gospel, all of you share in God's grace with me."
- 2 Timothy 4:16: "At my first *defense*, no one came to my support, but everyone deserted me. May it not be held against them."

Second, people need answers to the tough questions regarding the Christian faith. Many people simply will not accept Christianity as true without adequate evidence to support it. We live in a world of scams, junk email, and many who seek to deceive. An astute level of skepticism exists among many, requiring both a loving friendship and significant, compelling answers to bring people toward faith in Jesus Christ.

Third, history has shown that answering the questions people have about Christianity can help bring people to Christ. In addition to the examples shared in this chapter, I have experienced numerous people turning to faith in Christ as a result of providing answers to their faith questions. While belief in Christ is based on faith, it is not blind faith, but rather a reasonable faith that God expects when we come to him.

> "I believe Christianity is the only logical, consistent faith in the world."
>
> Mortimer Adler (1902–2001). Adler was editor of *Encyclopedia Britannica*, compiler of *Great Books of the Western World*, and though a self-described pagan for most of his life, became a Christian in the 1980s.

Christianity Is a Religion for the Educated

My friends Dr. Norm Geisler and Jason Jimenez note:

> Ravi Zacharias posits three tests that any statement or belief system must pass: (1) logical consistency (*Are there contradictions?*),

(2) empirical adequacy (*Is there any proof?*), and (3) experiential relevance (*Does it work in real life?*). For a statement or belief system to be logically consistent it must not contradict itself, but correspond to reality (that which is true). Moreover, the belief system must not only correspond to reality, but also cohere with the facts of reality (empirical adequacy). In other words, there must be evidence to substantiate its truth claims. And finally, a view or belief system must be viable to live by in the real world (experiential relevance). That is, its actions and values must comply with objective morality that we instinctively know is right.[12]

Many educated people have found that Christianity is credible, reasonable, and relevant. Skeptics present lots of tough questions about the Christian faith, yet for twenty years I have personally experienced people of all ages and backgrounds responding to caring, solid answers with deep appreciation.

One of the responses I often hear is, "Alex, all of this has helped me see that Christianity really makes sense." Don't write off faith as something only for the uneducated. I challenge you to consider the claims of Christianity and see for yourself whether you find it credible, reasonable, and relevant.

Myth #6

Christianity is boring and would be a waste of my time

Truth: Christianity is the most adventurous life a person can experience

"What would the world be like without God?" That was the subject of a debate I was asked to participate in with an atheist. The atheist's vision of a world without God was one free from the burden of religion, guilt over sin, or oppressive moral boundaries. My atheist opponent envisioned a glorious future without God, one in which humanity is finally free to explore human potential and at liberty to usher in a great utopia.

But is that what a future without God would really be?

Shawna has experienced a glimpse of a world without God. She has seen firsthand what results when ultimate truth is rejected and where moral boundaries no longer exist. For the last seven years Shawna has worked as a teacher in the Texas juvenile corrections system. She oversees a class of twenty-three girls for whom "public school is not an option."

Shawna told me, "During my first week a colleague said, 'Welcome to the jungle.' Fresh out of grad school, I had done practicums, but now working in the inner city full time, I really didn't know what I was in for." Shawna works with young girls who have been severely abused. "The kids we teach come from a world with no morals. There is nothing safe and no boundaries. I cannot describe what a culture of exploitation and abuse does to these children."

Shawna continued to explain that every one of her twenty-three female students had been sexually abused. It was hard to hear her describe one eight-year-old girl who was so violent to others that she had to be regularly physically restrained. The child had been gang raped and abused for an extended length of time. "This poor child was harmed virtually beyond description. Afterward, she would lash out and attempt to injure everyone who worked with her. The pain and wounds this child carries inside are just immeasurable."

> "There is often a sense of failure among professing Christians that is sadly out of keeping with their rightful position in Christ. Do not be overanxious. Live in your Father's house in constant freedom of heart. Remember that you are under the same roof as Christ, and are therefore allowed to avail yourself of all his grace and help. Refuse no task, however irksome, that God sets before you; and do not worry about irksome rules or petty vexations."
>
> F. B. Meyer (1847–1929), missionary in Europe, pioneered inner-city urban outreach

This is some of the fallout in a culture that has forgotten God. A world without God or objective morality, which many secularists work toward, creates a context in which the helpless are exploited and left broken. Those who believe the world would be better without God should look at the places today where he is most absent. Shawna would tell you the results speak for themselves.

Yet many today claim that being a Christian is a waste of time. Christianity is seen as boring, church is boring, and the Bible is boring. Even heaven is seen as one long church service—why would anyone want to go there? As a result, the compelling calling to "follow me" that Jesus presented is often lacking in our time.

In this chapter, we'll discuss all four of these common stereotypes about boring Christianity—the Christian faith, church, the Bible, and heaven—and show that an informed view of these areas reveals quite the opposite: Christianity is the most adventurous life a person can experience.

> "There was once in man a true happiness of which there now remain to him only the mark and empty trace, which he in vain tries to fill from all his surroundings. . . . But these are all inadequate, because the infinite abyss can only be filled by an infinite and immutable object, that is to say, only by God Himself. He only is our true good."
>
> Blaise Pascal (1623–1662), French philosopher and mathematician

"Being a Christian Is Boring"

You've probably heard these words. Perhaps you've even expressed them yourself. But are they true? If we look at the lives of those in the pews of some churches, we could be tempted to accept the myth that Christianity is indeed boring. But just because *some Christians* are boring doesn't mean that *Christianity* is boring. Let's look at the origin of the term and its earliest followers to see what Christianity is intended to be.

The first time the word *Christian* was used can be found in Acts 11:26: "So for a whole year Barnabas and Saul met with the church and taught great numbers of people. The disciples were called Christians first at Antioch." This term means "Christ followers" or "those belonging to Christ's party." The people who followed Jesus in this town were known for believing in Jesus as Lord and living like it.

Two of the key leaders in this Antioch church at the time were Paul and Barnabas. These two men led lives that were anything but boring. In Acts 13, God called these two men to leave Antioch and take the Good News of Jesus to new locations. They started numerous churches, performed miracles, endured persecution, and lived to tell about the adventure. The conclusion of their trip noted, "They preached the gospel in that city and won a large number of disciples" (Acts 14:21).

In addition to adventure and reaching many new people as missionaries, Paul often faced persecution. Second Corinthians 11:23–28 highlights:

> I have worked much harder, been in prison more frequently, been flogged more severely, and been exposed to death again and again. Five times I received from the Jews the forty lashes minus one. Three times I was beaten with rods, once I was pelted with stones, three times I was shipwrecked, I spent a night and a day in the open sea, I have been constantly on the move. I have been in danger from rivers, in danger from bandits, in danger from my fellow Jews, in danger from Gentiles; in danger in the city, in danger in the country, in danger at sea; and in danger from false believers. I have labored and toiled and have often gone without sleep; I have known hunger and thirst and have often gone without food; I have been cold and naked. Besides everything else, I face daily the pressure of my concern for all the churches.

While not always enjoyable, Paul's service as a Christian was anything but boring. He traveled thousands of miles, changed the lives of many people, and still today has left behind thirteen writings that are included in the New Testament and read by millions of people around the world each day.

The one other mention of the word *Christian* in the Bible is found in Acts 26:28. King Agrippa allowed Paul to defend himself, yet Paul took the opportunity to share his faith in Christ. The king replied, "Do you think that in such a short time you can persuade me to be a Christian?"

Paul replied, "Short time or long—I pray to God that not only you but all who are listening to me today may become what I am, except for these chains" (v. 29). Again, Paul stood before kings to share his faith. He endured suffering, imprisonment, and eventually death for the name of Christ.

Maybe you're thinking, *Yeah, but that was then. What about in my life, today?* The Jesus that Paul followed is the same Jesus Christians follow today. He was empowered by the same Holy Spirit who lives in all of Christ's followers. While Paul's calling as a missionary to the Gentiles was unique, his life serves as an example for the adventure available to followers of Christ.

In my own life, my parents expressed concern when I shared I would be serving God in vocational ministry rather than working in business or some other career. They too wondered how fulfilling such a life would be. Not long afterward, I had the opportunity to launch a nationwide campaign called "50 States in 50 Days." Over a fifty-day period, I became the first known minister to preach in all fifty U.S. states in just fifty days. The project sparked national news headlines and has served as a basis for much of my ministry since. My life has been anything but dull and boring.

I'm not alone or unique in this regard. The most motivated, fulfilled, joyful people I know are not those with the most wealth or celebrity status. Instead, they are men and women fulfilling God's call for their lives in all sorts of vocations, living for Jesus, sharing their faith, and changing lives both now and for eternity. As Jesus shared long ago, "I have come that they may have life, and have it to the full" (John 10:10).

"Church Is Boring"

Another common accusation about Christianity is that church is boring. To be fair, it would be accurate to say that many American churches are plateaued or are in decline. It is easy to understand why people would accuse the church of being boring based on their own experiences. However, that's not how church was meant to be. A look at the origin of the church provides a much different picture.

Following the launch of the church on the Day of Pentecost in the streets of Jerusalem, Acts 2:42–47 describes the practices of the first church:

> They devoted themselves to the apostles' teaching and to fellowship, to the breaking of bread and to prayer. Everyone was filled with awe at the many wonders and signs performed by the apostles. All the believers were together and had everything in common. They sold property and possessions to give to anyone who had need. Every day they continued to meet together in the temple courts. They broke bread in their homes and ate together with glad and sincere hearts, praising God and enjoying the favor of all the people. And the Lord added to their number daily those who were being saved.

Look at some of the traits mentioned in this original church:

- learning
- community
- shared meals
- prayer
- a sense of awe
- miracles
- sharing resources
- helping those in need

100

- daily gathering
- a good reputation with outsiders
- new people joining daily

This does not sound like a boring group of men and women, but rather a movement working to turn the world upside down (Acts 17:6).

My friend Dillon Burroughs shares in his book *Undefending Christianity*,

> Churches are like friends. They can bring great joy or great sorrow. It depends on which friend and at which moment we look. More accurately, churches *are* friends, connections of people who hold one common bond—the Son of God—whose blood was poured out for the doubters and despised, poor and wise.[1]

Today, churches are often viewed as a corporation rather than a congregation, an organization rather than an organism, and a monument rather than a movement. Yet God created the church as a family designed to communicate truth, build community, and change lives.

Popular professor and speaker Howard Hendricks was known for his comment that the church is often much like a professional football game. It consists of thousands of people watching a small number of people do all of the work. However, this was not the picture of the original church. Each person was important, involved, and active at a level of deep devotion. As Romans 12:15 teaches, the gathered believers should "rejoice with those who rejoice; mourn with those who mourn." When Peter was arrested and about to be put to death, the entire church gathered to pray for him throughout the night (Acts 12:5).

It has often been said that we are to be the change we wish to see in the world. The same is true with the church. Rather than complain about it or leave it, let us determine in our hearts to be the church we wish to see in the world. How can we "be the church" and make our local body of Christ a place of excitement and purpose?

Maybe you are a regular part of a body of believers, or perhaps you're visiting around in order to get some firsthand exposure to local churches. Great, either way! These next points are applicable for all who wish to be a part of what the New Testament calls *ekklesia* (the "called out" ones):

First, get in the game. There is no substitute for church involvement. It is much easier to complain from the sidelines, but when you become part of the solution, you are determined to make things better. Unfortunately, many believers have served in the past to the point of burnout or have been hurt in some other way and have opted to no longer try. While there are times a break or even a change of church may be necessary, there is no reason to quit the team.

Second, invest in your teammates. It is hard to complain about your church when they consist of your closest friends. The many "one another" commands of the New Testament remind us that the Christian life is not an individual sport but rather a team sport in which we all need to participate. When we make time to be with our Christian friends, encouraging one another, learning together, and serving together, church becomes something we do, not some thing we go to.

Third, pray for your church and its leaders. Your pastor and other church leaders have the extremely difficult job of helping your entire spiritual family grow in the faith. Take time each day to pray for your church's leaders. As you do, you may find your attitude toward them softening as well. You may desire to care for their needs and assist them rather than argue or gossip about problems in the church.

Fourth, contribute to your church. Yes, I know that financial giving to the church is not a fun topic. But here is what I've

102

discovered—I am more concerned about the causes to which I financially contribute. If I donate to a missionary's trip, I pray more for that person and am more interested in the project's outcome. The same is true of the local church. When we regularly give to our churches, we become more concerned that our contributions are being used wisely, and we eagerly want our congregations to grow. There is a direct correlation between our contributions to our churches and our care for our churches.

Fifth, invite someone to your church. If you do not feel comfortable inviting a new person to your main service, find an event or small group that would be more appropriate. When you begin seeking ways to involve new people, you begin to care more about the quality of your church's activities. It's similar to when you invite someone over to your home for dinner. Your house can be dirty all week, but when someone is coming to visit, you suddenly care much more about the way your home looks.

"The Bible Is Boring and Irrelevant to My Life"

I grew up in a church where the Bible teachings and prayers were filled with "thou," "shalt," and "thee." Much of Sunday's service often sounded more like a Shakespearian play than a message of hope. As a young person, it was easy to take from these experiences that the Bible was an ancient book that lacked any relevance to my life.

> "To fall in love with God is the greatest romance; to seek Him the greatest adventure; to find Him, the greatest human achievement."
>
> Augustine (AD 354–430)

It was not until years later that I began to discover the story of how the Bible came into existence and became familiar with its teachings. I found that it was not just another religious book full of do's and don'ts. I experienced the truth of the Bible's claim to be alive (Hebrews 4:12) and the very breath of God (2 Timothy 3:16).

Even for those who acknowledge the importance of the Bible, it can be a tough read. It's often difficult to figure out what it means or what to do with it. But I challenge you to give the Bible a chance before dismissing it. I want to share with you some of the habits that have helped me to find meaning in Scripture and stay sharp spiritually through reflecting on its principles.

First, prepare with prayer. When you attempt to understand what God is saying through the Bible, ask for wisdom. James 1:5 teaches, "If any of you lacks wisdom, you should ask God, who gives generously to all without finding fault, and it will be given to you."

Second, read from a translation that makes sense to you. Though some versions of the Bible are more literal than others, there is no perfect translation of the English Bible. The Scriptures were originally written in Hebrew, Aramaic, and Greek, not English. There are many quality Bible translations to choose from today. If you've tried to read the Bible but find it too difficult to understand, find another one that uses easier language to help bring the translation to life.

Third, read through books of the Bible instead of selected verses. Reading verses on a topic can be helpful, but it can also be confusing since each verse is found in a completely different context. Instead, focus on books of the Bible. You can begin with a short book like 1 John or Jonah and read it all at one time to understand both the big picture and the commands God has spoken.

Fourth, compare Scriptures on the same topic. While reading through books of the Bible is helpful for most study, additional insight can be found by reading several of the Bible's passages on the same topic. Unclear verses can often become more clear by comparing them with other verses. Use a concordance or Google to find lists of Bible verses on a particular topic. This ancient practice called the analogy of Scripture reveals that the Bible is ultimately its own best commentary.

Fifth, use additional resources sparingly. While I love to read, the numerous resources on our shelf or online can sometimes get in the way of actually reading the Bible. Use the Internet, Bible study software, or commentaries to help, but don't let them take the place of actually reading Scripture itself.

Sixth, don't trust only your feelings when reading Scripture. It can become very dangerous when we selectively read the Bible and "feel led" to do something without additional counsel or study. Such decisions have led to many theological and practical problems in which people assumed God wanted them to do something based on their own feelings without adequate study, prayer, and counsel with other believers.

Seven, apply what you read. It has been said that you believe only the parts of the Bible you live. While this is not exactly true, it can appear this way to those who watch your life. Make a conscience effort to implement something from your learning in order to make it real and relevant to your life situation. Some days may include only minor applications, while other days may include a complete life change, but there is always room to grow in our daily practice of God's Word.

"Heaven Sounds Like a Boring Place"

I'm always amazed when I hear someone say, "I don't know if I really want to go to heaven when I die. It sounds pretty boring." People who say this have clearly not understood the Bible's description of the Christian's eternal home.

First, Christians will be with the Lord. The apostle Paul said, "I desire to depart and be with Christ, which is better by far" (Philippians 1:23). In 2 Corinthians 5:8 he wrote, "We are confident, I say, and would prefer to be away from the body

Christianity dull? Not for these two believers.

David Brainerd (1718–1747) was a frontier missionary to Native Americans. Born in Connecticut, Brainerd attended Yale University to prepare for ministry but was kicked out. The famed pastor/theologian/evangelist Jonathan Edwards published Brainerd's diaries in 1749. People had told Brainerd, "Those savages will kill you." But Brainerd went into the wilderness, learned the language, lived among the Native Americans, and in the first year, seventy came to faith. Brainerd died at twenty-nine of tuberculosis. His short but significant life deeply influenced a man named William Carey (1761–1834).

William Carey—born in England—was a sixteen-year-old shoemaker. As he read the Bible, Carey became convinced that it was the church's job to take the gospel of Jesus to all people. At the time, this was a radical idea. During William Carey's lifetime in England, the common view was that "Great Commission" verses like Matthew 28:18–20 or Mark 16:15 had applied only to the generation of Christ's original apostles. There was little emphasis on world missions, and talk of a Great Commission made minimal impact within the church.

As Carey began to talk about taking the message of Jesus to the world, his family—even his wife—thought he was a fanatic. Carey had become pastor of a Baptist church, and he eventually announced that God had called him to take the Gospel to India. His wife and family fought this dream.

Carey's three actions used greatly by God

In spite of opposition from those closest to him, Carey was determined. He eventually preached what some say is one of the most influential sermons of all time. Some believe that the influence of this sermon is second only to Peter's sermon at Pentecost. Cary delivered a message titled, "Expect Great Things From God—Attempt Great Things For God." The vision and faith of the hearers was immeasurably expanded.

Second, Carey wrote a book (with a title that may sound strange to our ears): *An Enquiry Into the Obligation of Christians to Use Means for the Conversion of the Heathen.* The book's impact has been compared to that of Martin Luther's Ninety-five Theses.

Third, Carey went to India in spite of the fact that family and friends were highly critical and resistant. While in India, he learned native languages and translated the entire Bible into six different languages and parts of Scriptures into twelve other languages. Carey's sermon, book, and missionary zeal not only touched India (where he was serving) but also Britain and most of Europe.

God used this man (and his inspiration, David Brainerd) to remind the whole church of its obligation to proclaim Jesus to the world. William Carey would ultimately be remembered as "The Father of Modern Missions." Not so dull after all!

and at home with the Lord." He knew his eternal home would be far superior to his earthly life. First Thessalonians 4:17 explains that when this life is over, "We will be with the Lord forever." There is no greater place to be than with the Creator and Savior for eternity.

Second, Christians will receive new bodies. For many, it is a blessing to know that they will have new bodies in heaven. Second Corinthians 5:1 teaches, "For we know that if the earthly tent we live in is destroyed, we have a building from God, an eternal house in heaven, not built by human hands." Evangelist Billy Graham said, "Heavenly rest will be so refreshing that we will never feel that exhaustion of mind and body we so frequently experience now. I'm really looking forward to that."[2]

Third, heaven will be completely free from sin. In the new heaven, God promises, "No longer will there be any curse. The throne of God and of the Lamb will be in the city, and his servants will serve him" (Revelation 22:3). The frustrating temptations that pressure us each day in this life will no longer exist.

Fourth, there will be a perfect existence. Revelation 22:1–2 provides a glimpse of the new heaven that will serve as the ultimate resting place of all believers in Christ:

> Then the angel showed me the river of the water of life, as clear as crystal, flowing from the throne of God and of the Lamb down the middle of the great street of the city. On each side of the river stood the tree of life, bearing twelve crops of fruit, yielding its fruit every month. And the leaves of the tree are for the healing of the nations.

Fifth, Christians will be reunited with all of God's people. One of the reasons I most anticipate heaven is the opportunity to be reunited with those who have died in Christ before me. I will enjoy heaven with Abraham, Isaac, Jacob, and Moses. I will meet David, Sarah, Ruth, Mary, Peter, Paul, and so many others I've read about in Scripture. I will meet the known as well as unknown saints from the centuries, from Augustine to Martin Luther, from the first missionaries to China to those who first translated the Scriptures to remote tribes in Papua New Guinea.

Personally, I'll be looking forward to eternity with my believing family members who have passed on before me. We "do not grieve like the rest of mankind, who have no hope" (1 Thessalonians 4:13). I know there will be a day when I will once again meet face-to-face with every friend and family member in Christ who has departed before me. The Christian mother will be reunited with her daughter who died in miscarriage. The son will be reunited with his Christian father who died in military service. Children will be reunited with their godly grandparents who prayed for them and loved them as children. If only for this reason, heaven is a time to look forward to like none other!

Sam Storms offers a moving personal illustration of the power of heaven:

> A friend of mine, whom I'll call "Steve," suffered the loss of his young wife after only two years of marriage. Not long after, he was diagnosed with multiple sclerosis. As he tried to make sense of his tragic past and the frustrations of the present, his confident hope of future glory sustained him on a daily basis (2 Corinthians 4:16–18). His inescapable suffering was bearable only as he embraced an eternal perspective. He regarded the afflictions of his "present" as minor when compared with the weight of the glory yet to come. Steve found the key to endurance when he took the long view. Only when he looked upon the hardships of this life in the light of endless ages of eternal bliss was he empowered to persevere and even rejoice.[3]

Ultimately, it is our focus that is the problem. As author Randy Alcorn explains:

Nothing is more often misdiagnosed than our homesickness for Heaven. We think that what we want is sex, drugs, alcohol, a new job, a raise, a doctorate, a spouse, a large-screen television, a new car, a cabin in the woods, a condo in Hawaii. What we really want is the person we were made for, Jesus, and the place we were made for, Heaven. Nothing less can satisfy us.[4]

Choose for Yourself

It has been said that some people aren't very excited about heaven because they are far too in love with this world. It is generally in our darkest moments that we long for heaven the most. If you focus only on reaching the next paycheck, the next goal, or the next weekend, it is hard to look forward to heaven. The best way to become more excited about heaven is to live for eternity today. When your life is consumed with living for Jesus and sharing him with others, heaven will be what you live for and long for.

Myth #7

Christianity isn't real because it didn't work for me

Truth: The Christian faith is difficult, yet also the most rewarding way of life

Stephanie's dad was a pastor in a small rural community. She grew up among friendly neighbors, sang in the youth choir, and attended a local school small enough for just about everyone to be on a first-name basis. She could not imagine a future anything less than the idyllic life she had always known.

A harsh reality began to insert itself when her dad walked out on his marriage of thirty years and pastorate of fifteen years. Stephanie's family was devastated, and the little community watched in shock as a trusted "man of God" left his wife for one of the church members. "I saw my father say and do things that I would have never thought possible," Stephanie said. "The affair, their appearances together in public—it was so painful for our family, embarrassing for the church, and it just rocked our community."

Deeply painful situations that come on people abruptly become defining moments. How a person processes such circumstances shapes him for years to come. For a "preacher's kid" in her late teens, Stephanie's situation could have been what I call "spiritually terminal." Emerging from the rubble of life's implosions leaves some as bitter skeptics.

Stephanie said, "I remember lying on the floor just wishing I could die. I felt anger toward my dad and anger toward God. But eventually I realized that this was not God's fault. My dad made the decision to walk away. I realized I now had to make a decision in light of my dad's decision."

As the agonizing months of a family breakup dragged on, Stephanie began to understand that her reaction to it all would profoundly shape her future. She says,

> I asked myself, "Will I, like my dad, turn my back on my faith, my life, and all I knew to be true?" This became the defining moment of my life, so far. I was hurting, but at the same time I knew that many facts affirm that Christianity is true. Jesus Christ *did* live, die, and rise again. Looking back, I remembered times that God had answered prayer and provided for my needs. The healing of my emotions began when I made the mental choice to trust God even in this deep valley. As I made the decision to trust God, I felt His presence as never before. Even though some days are still emotionally challenging, the sense of peace God gave me has never left, and my walk with Christ has grown stronger since then.[1]

"The Christian ideal has not been tried and found wanting. It has been found difficult; and left untried."

G. K. Chesterton
(1874–1936)

Stephanie's story is a good example of how to process one's pain in a way that is both redemptive and healthy. But it could have become an example of the many who are spiritually wounded and use these wounds as a reason to turn away from God.

"It Didn't Work for Me"

Maybe you've expressed these words or heard them from someone you know. There are times when the Christian life is tough and can make us feel like giving up. In fact, many do. Repeated studies show that many of the Christian teenagers in America are leaving their faith as they head to college campuses. Why is this the case?

One of the major reasons I hear in my events on college campuses across the nation is that Christianity lacks relevance in their lives or that they have been hurt by a Christian along the way. Many have decided it is better to go through life without God than to give him another chance. Dayna Drum writes in *Relevant* magazine,

> There are a lot of issues the Church doesn't talk about. We allow these unspoken problems to sit alongside us like regular members of the congregation, and refuse to acknowledge them. Spiritual abuse is one of these issues that has been sitting uncomfortably ignored in the back pews of our churches. Usually, we either act like it isn't happening or run from it, sometimes abandoning the Church altogether because of an unhealthy situation.
>
> But the time is long overdue for the Church to start talking about and confronting spiritual abuse.[2]

Psalm 38:11 reveals, "My friends and companions avoid me because of my wounds; my neighbors stay far away." In this chapter, I want to address the myth that Christianity is bad or somehow wrong because it didn't work out for you. I want to begin by sharing some of the types of wounds I've seen in my efforts to share Christ.

Church Wounds

The first type of wounds people often experience are what I call church wounds. Those of you who have been raised in the church probably know what I mean. Church can be tough, possibly leaving some with a sort of post-traumatic church disorder. In some cases, the scandal of a church leader can destroy an entire congregation. When those we trust in ministry betray us, it is extremely difficult to trust again. One of my friends attended a church in which an elder had embezzled a half million dollars from his church over a period of time. The church has taken years to rebuild trust regarding the financial giving of its members.

In other cases, the problem is a moral scandal. A youth pastor sleeps with a teenage girl in his group. A pastor's family splits over infidelity. The scenarios differ, but the end result is the same—trust is broken and wounds are left.

Some church wounds arise from the pride or abuse of authority by church leaders. When a church leader uses people to accomplish his or her own success in ministry, it soon becomes evident to the members. From an unhealthy emphasis on clothing, cars, or financial gain, to repeated talk about numbers and statistical success, ministerial pride can leave deep wounds and destroy entire congregations.

Some church wounds are not about finances, sexual immorality, or pride, but result from the betrayal of confidential information. In another book, I share about a girl named Andrea who was highly involved in her church's youth group, yet at the age of seventeen she began to struggle with same-sex attraction. Though she had never acted on these attractions, she confided in her youth pastor, asking for his prayers and counsel.

Her plea for help backfired. The youth minister somehow considered Andrea a threat to the youth group and publicly told the parents of all of the other teenagers. Andrea was horrified.

She left the church and five years later was still struggling with the ability to trust enough to even participate in church again.[3]

Church members aren't the only ones to face wounds; church leaders do as well. One pastor whose story I read even shared:

> I remember the exact point I hit bottom. I was staring into a bathroom mirror with a bottle of sleeping pills in my hand. A voice of reason began to speak . . . but a second voice interrupted, "Don't think, just swallow. Don't think, just swallow."
>
> And I did.
>
> I assumed one bottle of prescription sleeping pills would do it. But just in case, I pulled out a second bottle and gulped those down as well.
>
> The next few hours are a blur. But I do recall my wife sitting next to me in the hospital. And I can see her face as she said through tears, "We're going to get through this."[4]

Many church leaders face burnout, stress, and other burdens related to ministry at various levels. As I communicate with ministry leaders nationwide, I often find wounds from years of overextending one's health, family, and relational abilities to unhealthy levels.

When churches or ministries become places of emotional wounding, a tragically negative witness is imprinted on the memories of people. Anne Graham Lotz (daughter of famed evangelist Billy Graham) penned *Wounded by God's People* (Zondervan, 2013) in response to this. I have met many who, after having endured some "toxic faith" experience, assume that Christianity must be false. But Jesus is alive and authentic, even if many who use his name don't live up to biblical standards in their treatment of others. Believers are not calling the world to believe in a *Christian* who may let you down, but on *Christ,* who will *never* leave nor forsake you (Hebrews 13:5).

Even if every Christian failed to model Christlikeness, that would not negate the reality of God and the gospel. The factual

> "Faith is to believe what we do not see, and the reward of this faith is to see what we believe."
>
> Augustine (AD 354–430)

nature of the gospel does not hang on the behavior of Christians (thankfully!). However, Christians do well to be mindful that a watching world is evaluating the worth and truth of the message based on our lives. The Christian community should not leave a toxic residue on the lives of people. While the Bible speaks of giving up certain things to serve in ministry, there is a line between personal commitment and sacrificing personal health, physical and spiritual, which is sometimes crossed during the course of ministry.

Relational Wounds

A second area consists of relational wounds. When a relationship with a family member, friend, or church leader turns ugly as a result of events connected with our faith, people often respond by leaving the church or their faith completely. When I speak with young people who have left the church, I often ask what led them to abandon their spiritual family. Many times the answer has nothing to do with beliefs, but more to do with people. When Christ's followers resemble little of the Christ they claim to serve, those watching often flee from both these superficial followers and from God.

Another concern often deals with how Christians respond to those who differ from their beliefs. While we are to speak the truth, we are called to do so in love (Ephesians 4:15). Unfortunately, this is not always the case. For example, one young woman shared, "I am posting this because my parents don't know I'm Wiccan, and I know a few people that keep it from everyone apart from their closest friends or other Wiccans. I don't tell my parents because they don't need to know and I wouldn't want them to jump to conclusions about it and judge it now. I may tell them in the future and I may tell everyone I meet in the future about it but for now I am fine as I am."[5]

This young woman, raised in a Christian home, secretly practiced witchcraft. She refused to tell her parents or many others about it for fear of how they would treat her. While Christian parents would understandably be concerned about their teenager becoming involved in another religion, there was certainly also a relational barrier that kept this young woman and her parents from open communication about spiritual beliefs and practices.

In other cases, the concern is not another religion but the Christian culture in which a person is raised. Some gifted musicians are raised in churches in which musical instruments are completely banned, leading to various conflicts. Other churches have wrongly discriminated against those in their church and community because of hair length, a nose ring, tattoo, or some other external factor that was somehow considered socially unacceptable. James 2:2–4 directly addresses this issue, saying,

> Suppose a man comes into your meeting wearing a gold ring and fine clothes, and a poor man in filthy old clothes also comes in. If you show special attention to the man wearing fine clothes and say, "Here's a good seat for you," but say to the poor man, "You stand there" or "Sit on the floor by my feet," have you not discriminated among yourselves and become judges with evil thoughts?

In another passage, Samuel was called to anoint one of the sons of Jesse as the next king of Israel. When the oldest son stood before him, Samuel thought, "Surely the Lord's anointed stands here before the Lord" (1 Samuel 16:6). But God replied, "Do not consider his appearance or his height, for I have rejected him. The Lord does not look at the things people look at. People look at the outward appearance, but the Lord looks at the heart" (v. 7). God teaches we are to avoid discrimination and favoring people by their appearances. Whether a person sports a mohawk or a suit and tie on Sunday morning communicates far less than a heart that pursues the Lord.

The story of Borgland Baptist Church is another example.[6] For more than ten years, Borgland Baptist had been a vibrant congregation. The pastor was a highly visible figure in the community, known for visiting the sick and elderly. When a scandal involving the pastor and key leaders made the local news, the congregation quickly divided. The scandal included sex, power, money, and a homicide that resulted in legal charges against the pastor and several church members. The church soon completely closed, leaving nothing but a vacant building as a memory of its former days. While this church is an extreme example, it illustrates the impact of a few Christians displaying poor relationships that wound others. When relationships are broken, the damage leaves a large and lasting impact.

When circumstances leave previously close friends divided, the pain can be especially long-lasting. I think of an attorney who came to me for pastoral counseling regarding an unpleasant encounter from his college days. Robert explained that he was an agnostic—he wasn't sure if God existed and didn't think anyone could know. In the course of our conversations about faith and the evidence for Christianity, Robert stated that he had once considered himself a Christian believer.

While attending law school, some friends who were professed Christians urged Robert to stop being friends with a student who was Jewish (who also happened to be Robert's roommate in the dorm). The anti-Semitism of supposed Christians at first confused Robert, then left him angry. When the others students' aversion to the Jewish roommate turned to vocal abuse and harassment, Robert sided with his friend—and *against* belief in God.

"I couldn't believe that these same students who were faithful in their attendance at chapel services could be so hurtful toward a fellow human being," Robert said. "I thought, *If Christianity has room for this kind of hate, I want no part of it.*" The whole episode was painful to hear about, and yet my heart sank even further when I learned that all of this took place more than thirty years ago. After years of confirmed agnosticism, Robert still had a desire to believe in God, yet struggled with how to understand a heart of hate in the lives of professed Christians. My conversations with Robert showed that decades of time had not at all resolved the conflict associated with this. Such is the depth of relational wounds.

Theological Wounds

Other wounds arise when inaccurate beliefs are perpetuated in a family or a church. For example, some are taught that they lose their salvation whenever they sin against God. As a result, I've prayed with students for their salvation, later to discover they keep "asking Jesus into their heart" every Sunday to make sure they go to heaven. This is *not* the gospel Jesus gave. John said, "I write these things to you who believe in the name of the Son of God so that you may know that you have eternal life" (1 John 5:13).

Others have been wrongly taught that a Christian who commits suicide automatically goes to hell. Could you imagine hearing this as a parent whose child has just committed such an act? There is no verse in the Bible that says this. While suicide is never the answer, it is important that we teach what Scripture teaches and not more. I know from personally counseling people over the years that untold damage has resulted from this one theological wound. We are called to "mourn with those who mourn" (Romans 12:15), not to spread unhealthy teachings to those already hurting.

119

I've heard many other wrong theological views turn people from God and the church as well. Whether it's telling people they have sinned for voting differently than expected, to excommunicating members over the translation of the Bible they use, to the emotional extremes of some churches that take priority over biblical truth, many have fled congregations as the result of poor theology that has left a trail of injured souls.

Emotional Wounds

I find it fascinating that some of those most angry at God are those who do not believe he exists. For example, Joe Carter wrote in the online publication *First Things*,

> I've shaken my fist in anger at stalled cars, storm clouds, and incompetent meteorologists. I've even, on one terrible day that included a dead alternator, a blaring tornado-warning siren, and a horrifically wrong weather forecast, cursed all three at once. I've fumed at furniture, cussed at crossing guards, and held a grudge against Gun Barrel City, Texas. I've been mad at just about anything you can image. Except unicorns. I've never been angry at unicorns.[7]

"I want you to dismantle Christianity for me. Tell me why there is no God."

With that question—phrased in basically that way nearly three dozen times—I began to interview professed atheists for what was to be a single book on unbelief. What resulted were *two* books, each slightly nuanced in order to try to adequately address their respective topics: The first book was *10 Answers for Skeptics*, the second was *10 Answers for Atheists*.

Actually, each book attempted to provide dozens of answers to dozens of questions. It was my privilege to sit down with well-known atheists such as the late Christopher Hitchens, David Silverman of American Atheists, Michael Shermer of *Skeptic* magazine, with Bible critic Bart Ehrman, and others. My research team and I made a very sincere effort to provide substantive responses to actual issues and objections raised by the unbelievers interviewed. (The "10" part related to the fact that I uncovered what I believe were specific *profiles* of skeptics and atheists.)

The conversations revealed that unbelief manifests itself differently in different lives, but there are clearly some specific patterns that appear. Interestingly, of the nearly three dozen atheists/agnostics/skeptics with whom I had conversation, most had some type of church or religious background. Michael Shermer had been in Campus Crusade for Christ during the "Jesus Movement" of the 1970s. Bart Ehrman (who now claims that there are some 100,000 errors in the Bible) had worked with the youth in his church. Twenty-eight of the skeptics I interviewed were ex-Protestants. Four were ex-Roman Catholics.

Having heart-to-heart conversations with unbelievers from many walks of life revealed to me that virtually all were, essentially, *ex-believers*. And if one thing was undeniably clear, the state of ex-belief came about due to *pain*. "Where was God when my mother was dying of cancer? We prayed in Jesus' name, asking for her to be healed. . . ." "My father was a leader in the church, and he abused us. . . ." "Our preacher was very demanding, authoritarian, and yet it became known that he was committing immorality within the church and stealing the tithes and offerings. . . ."

Over and over I heard heart-wrenching stories about circumstances gone wrong, Christians behaving badly, and broken hearts left in the wake. And it seemed that as people looked back on painful seasons of life, they limped toward the conclusion that God had just not come through. Prayers were prayed, verses were quoted, and yet life still imploded. Where was God in all of this? "Perhaps . . . maybe . . . there is no God." This seemed to be the often-repeated line of thought.

Now, many of the skeptics with whom I spoke propped up their unbelief with sophisticated-sounding arguments: Darwin, evolution, philosophical issues, the problem of pain and suffering in the world, the hypocrisy of other Christians, problems with the Bible, etc. But through personal interviews and also through taking hundreds of on-air phone calls in fifteen years of talk radio, I have firmly come to the following conclusion: **Intellectual skepticism is preceded by emotional pain.** Intellectual doubt comes second—in most cases. The road to rejection of God *begins* with emotional pain, leading one to question if God is even real, or whether God truly cares.

> "But whatever you do, find the God-centered, Christ-exalting, Bible-saturated passion of your life, and find your way to say it and live for it and die for it. And you will make a difference that lasts. You will not waste your life."
>
> Pastor/author
> John Piper, *Don't Waste Your Life*

I told one atheist friend, "You talk about God more than any preacher I know!" It dawned on me that the atheists I know don't merely ignore God; they seem *angry* at him. "Well, I am angry," said one atheist with whom I spoke. "I am angry that most of the world believes some cosmic guy in the sky is running things. I want to deliver them from that delusion."

But we humans can't be *passionless* about the most core questions of life. The atheists' activism, their feeling that they are somehow *called* on a mission to "save" the world from God, amounts to a religious fervor. This strikes me as odd, in a universe that is supposedly free from any divine causes or purposes. . . . If there is no God, why the vehement emotion against him? Why feel the need to crusade against religion? Why not just live, be happy, and one day return to the primordial matter of which Darwin wrote?

During a debate with Christopher Hitchens in 2008, the famed atheist spent much time insisting that he was free of belief. He wanted to make it clear that his atheism was "the absence of belief" (many atheists with whom I speak are careful to point this out). But in closing statements, as the audience asked questions about how the world *ought* to be, Hitchens a couple of times caught himself saying, "I believe . . ." The audience laughed as he corrected himself. The second or third time he accidentally began a sentence with, "My beliefs . . ." and then quickly grasped for another word (he finished the debate saying, "My conviction is this . . . My conviction is that . . ."), it became clear that there is no real absence of belief. We *will* believe in something, and that belief will motivate us to act in certain ways.

None of us has a heart that is a purely blank page. The atheist, however articulately they may rail against God, is in fact expressing a type of belief. Life's tough circumstances may lead one to question whether or not God cares, or is even real. But belief in God is the "default" position of the human heart. In response to pain, we construct (and later defend) systems of anti-belief in our minds.

The Great Physician

Sometimes the wounds we incur—which may later fuel rejection of God or abandonment of faith altogether—may come from the church. Well-intentioned but misguided Christians in our lives may say and do things that cut us deeply and may shake our faith in Christ significantly. Author and speaker Mary De-Muth offers some of her experiences regarding spiritual abuse that many Christians can relate to in their own lives regarding emotional wounds. They include:

- A leader telling me that even though I was burned out and losing my health, I had to stay in the ministry because if I didn't I would lose all my gifting for future ministry.

- A church that repeatedly told us they basically had the corner on the market of Jesus and that if we had to go elsewhere, we would miss God's highest.

- A leader who found ministry to be a vehicle for his great gain, lying and manipulating donors to earn more and more money.

- A ministry that shamed me into throwing away all my evil music (including Lionel Ritchie and Duran Duran . . . Oh, the evil!).

- A leader who cornered me, threatened me, and yelled because I brought up a concern that others saw. This led to panic attacks.[8]

While these and other wounds are real and painful, they are not the end of the journey. The Lord is the Great Physician who can heal our wounds and offer a corrective to the myth that Christianity "didn't work for me." Though Christians or a local church may fail us at times, Christ never fails. If you or someone you know has left the faith due to past wounds, let me encourage you to do the following.

First, rediscover the true Jesus. You may have been taught that Jesus hates gay people and those who can't quit smoking. The truth is that Jesus came to seek and to save the lost. He "did not come to be served, but to serve, and to give his life as a ransom for many" (Matthew 20:28). I challenge you to open the gospel of John and begin reading with eyes that seek the true, biblical Jesus. When you do, you may discover he is much different from the Jesus you have been told about in your painful past experiences.

Second, realize that not every person who claims to follow Jesus represents him well. Instead of fleeing from Christians because of those who are toxic, seek believing friends who truly desire to live according to God's ways. Even one or two genuine Christian friends are enough community to begin to change your life in a positive direction.

Third, restart your walk with a new life in Christ. Yes, your past may have been painful, even in the church or in a Christian family. Today can be different. Second Corinthians 5:17 reminds us, "If anyone is in Christ, the new creation has come: The old has gone, the new is here!" You can begin today with new patterns that help you move forward in a life of faith based on the true message of Christ.

> "Without faith it is impossible to please God, because anyone who comes to him must believe that he exists and that he rewards those who earnestly seek him."
>
> Hebrews 11:6

Fourth, refocus on serving others. One of the best ways to get out of spiritual neutral is to help someone else in need. Find a local soup kitchen, after-school program, nursing home, prison outreach, or other effort where you can use your time and abilities to make a difference in the lives of others. Matthew 10:39 teaches, "Whoever finds their life will lose it, and whoever loses their life for my sake will find it." True Christianity is based on loving God and serving others.

On a related note, some who have been spiritually wounded have never left the church. Maybe you have been hurt but have chosen to remain, press on, and act like nothing happened. This response may not be the healthiest way to deal with your pain. While serving others is admirable, give yourself permission to take a break and be less involved for a period of time. *Busyness is not equal to godliness.* The best thing for your life may be a period of rest, reminding yourself of the words of Psalm 23:1–4:

> The Lord is my shepherd, I lack nothing.
> He makes me lie down in green pastures,

he leads me beside quiet waters,
> he refreshes my soul.
He guides me along the right paths
> for his name's sake.
Even though I walk
> through the darkest valley,
I will fear no evil,
> for you are with me;
your rod and your staff,
> they comfort me.

Fifth, remember to forgive as you have been forgiven. Jesus taught in the Lord's Prayer, "And forgive us our debts, as we also have forgiven our debtors" (Matthew 6:12). Living for Christ includes forgiveness of those who have harmed you. Though difficult and perhaps an issue that takes time, your full restoration to living for God will include extending forgiveness to those who have hurt you in the past.

Myth #8

Christianity is false because it is based on the Bible, which is filled with errors and contradictions

Truth: The Bible is the most accurately preserved book in history

In his bestselling book *Forged*, Dr. Bart Ehrman, professor of religion at the University of North Carolina, Chapel Hill, writes, "Eventually I came to realize that the Bible not only contains untruths or accidental mistakes. It also contains what almost anyone today would call lies."[1] Is he right? Has the Bible communicated errors and contradictions that should cause us to consider it unworthy of our attention regarding matters of faith and spirituality? If not, how do we know that the Bible is a God-inspired book?

The Bible was written by at least forty authors over a 1,500-year period, and yet the sixty-six books carry a unified message of God's love and salvation. Volumes have been written about the Bible's unique characteristics, including its apparent inde-structibility and its historical, scientific, and prophetic truths. The trustworthiness of Scripture is clearly addressed internally. The Bible states, "Your word, Lord, is eternal" (Psalm 119:89), "Every word of God is flawless" (Proverbs 30:5), and "The Scrip-ture cannot be broken" (John 10:35 NKJV). But to quit there would leave us staking eternity on circular reasoning. You and I both want more evidence than "It's true because it says it's true." Fortunately, other facts testify on behalf of the Bible's accuracy.

Has the Bible Been Accurately Preserved?

By historical standards, the Old Testament is very accurate. As Jewish scribes made copies of those Scriptures, they counted the letters on each page—forward and backward, on the master copy and the new edition—to ensure that nothing was added or omitted. Though the Old Testament comes to us through a comparatively fewer number of known manuscripts than the New Testament, the books have been meticulously preserved. In fact, a copy of Isaiah found among the Dead Sea Scrolls and dated to about 200 BC was virtually identical to the next oldest copy we have, which is dated to around AD 900. That's 1,100 years of faithful transmission on this book alone.

Confidence in the New Testament lies in the amazing number of copies discovered. In addition to the books themselves, more than 86,000 quotations of individual verses by early Christians have been found. They date from within 150 to 200 years of the time of Christ and dramatically illustrate the familiarity that ancient Christians had with the New Testament Scriptures.

Comparing the New Testament with secular writings from the ancient world, the Bible's closest peer could be Homer's *The*

Iliad, a manuscript existing in more than six hundred copies. Homer beats Aristotle but still can't hold a candle to the Bible. The number of ancient texts containing all or part of the New Testament number around 30,000.

Is what we have now really what was in the Bible originally? Yes, we can trust on pretty good authority that the Bible we have today corresponds to the original texts. We have thousands of complete and partial manuscripts of the Bible dated very close to the actual events, and except for minor textual differences, none of which affects a major doctrine, there is remarkable similarity between ancient and modern texts.

Is the Bible Reliable?

The book of Acts cites at least eighty-four historical facts verified by later research and archaeology. Luke's accuracy regarding details, names, and places has been acknowledged by numerous historians. This same author also mentions thirty-five miracles in Acts. Why would Luke have been meticulously accurate in his history and misleading when talking of other things? Indeed, Scripture is dependable for its statements about history and destiny, the physical world, and spiritual realities.

> "There are more sure marks of authenticity in the Bible than in any profane [secular] history."
>
> Physicist Isaac Newton (1643–1727)

Our view of Scripture should be in harmony with that of Jesus. Christ affirmed the Old Testament (Matthew 5:18; Luke 24:44) and made provision for the soon-to-come New Testament (John 14:26). These facts, when taken together, point out that an all-powerful God certainly could create such a document, but is it reasonable to accept that he did? The external evidence, the Bible itself, and the risen Jesus all say yes.

Who Decided Which Books Would Be Included in the Bible?

The short answer: God did. God is the author of all Scripture, and the Bible is the collection of that Scripture. Perhaps a better question is this: How were those books recognized and collected?

The collecting of the manuscripts that now make up the Holy Bible occurred as books were circulated among the people of God and recognized as Scripture. Scholars call this *canonization* (from *canon*, the Latin word for "measuring stick"). The early church leaders did not "choose" the canon. They recognized the books that God had chosen.

Five principles guided this process. Early church leaders considered these aspects of a given text according to the following criteria.

First, does it have the authority of God? There may be authoritative claims about how a believer should live or what God has done. There may be an explicit claim: "Thus says the Lord." In some form, the book will claim the authority of God.

Second, was it written by a servant of God? The author may have been a prophet or apostle, or have been sponsored by one.

Third, does it tell the truth about God? Does its content harmonize with other known Scripture? All Scripture is without error. If a book contained factual errors or contradicted other Scripture, it would fail this test.

Fourth, does it display the power of God? True Scripture has the power to change lives and build up the people of God.

Fifth, is it accepted by the people of God? The book had to be accepted by the people of God to whom it was initially given.

There was some disagreement about a few of the books, but even very early on, the church and church fathers were using as authoritative the books we find in our Bibles today. In 367, Bishop Athanasius of Alexandria listed the books he thought should be included in the Bible, and his list corresponds exactly to those found in Protestant Bibles today. (The Roman Catholic Church and some Eastern Orthodox churches include books not included in the Protestant Bible.)

Why Trust the Bible?

Okay, the manuscripts that make up the Bible may be accurately preserved and contain reliable facts, but that doesn't necessarily mean they were supernaturally inspired. How can we be so sure that the Bible was given by God?

The Bible claims to be the Word of God (Psalms 93:5; 119:89; Proverbs 30:5; Matthew 24:35; John 10:35; 2 Timothy 3:16). If that were all the evidence, though, you'd be right to be skeptical of such a claim. But the divine origin of the Bible is confirmed though numerous historical accounts that are verified

> "After more than two centuries of facing the heaviest scientific guns that could be brought to bear, the Bible has survived. . . . The Scriptures seem more acceptable now than they did when the rationalists began the attack."
>
> *Time* magazine

by other sources, many fulfilled prophecies, and the unity of sixty-six books written over a period of 1,500 years by multiple authors from several cultures.

The first reason we can trust the Bible is its fulfilled prophecies. Hundreds of specific prophecies have been fulfilled, often long after the prophetic writer had passed away. For example, the prophet Daniel predicted around 538 BC in Daniel 9:24–27 that Christ would come as Israel's promised Savior and prince 483 years after the Persian emperor would give the Jews authority to rebuild Jerusalem. At the time of the prophecy, Jerusalem was in ruins. Yet this was clearly fulfilled hundreds of years later in Jesus.

The Bible is full of extensive prophecies dealing with individual nations and cities as well as the course of history in general, all of which have been literally fulfilled. More than three hundred prophecies were fulfilled by Christ's first coming. Other prophecies deal with a wide variety of subjects, including the spread of Christianity and of various false religions.

Mathematics and astronomy professor Peter Stoner was a skeptic of the Bible. To test its prophetic accuracy (which is often considered a test of any major religion), he observed forty-eight major Old Testament prophecies concerning the Messiah who would come. Out of these forty-eight, he considered just eight of these dealing with the Messiah being born in Bethlehem, his persecution, the attempts on his life, and others that established several parameters to govern who this Messiah would be. Using the principles of probability, he concluded the following: The chance that any man might have lived and fulfilled all eight prophecies is one in 10 followed by 17 zeros. Yet the chance that any one man fulfilled all forty-eight prophecies is an astounding one in 10 followed by 157 zeros.[2]

This example neither proves nor disproves Jesus was the Messiah, nor that the Bible is true. But it does highlight that the Bible stands in a separate category from other religious and spiritual books. The prophecies of the Bible, unlike the predictions of other religions, are both specific and verifiable.

There is no other book, ancient or modern, with these sorts of specific and verifiable prophecies that have come to pass. Compared with the vague prophecies of today's spiritual gurus, only the Bible manifests this remarkable prophetic evidence, and it does so on such a tremendous scale that it could only be explained by divine revelation.

A second reason we can trust the Bible is from God is its historical accuracy. Archaeological confirmations, for example, have revealed thousands of accurate statements about geography, towns, locations, and customs of ancient history. While there are a small number of people and places that so far have no extra-biblical reference, there are no known inaccuracies in the Bible.

A third reason we can trust that the Bible is God's Word is its scientific accuracy. Long before scientists had discovered such data, many scientific facts had been recorded in Scripture. Among them include:

- The roundness of the earth (Isaiah 40:22)
- The law of conservation of mass and energy (2 Peter 3:7)
- The hydrologic cycle (Ecclesiastes 1:7)
- The vast number of stars (Jeremiah 33:22)
- The law of increasing entropy (Psalm 102:25–27)
- The importance of blood to life (Leviticus 17:11)
- Atmospheric circulation (Ecclesiastes 1:6)
- The gravitational field (Job 26:7)

The Bible is not a science textbook, but it does speak accurately when it notes aspects of the natural world. While the Bible does not explain all there is to know about the created world, it does offer an accurate description of our world, as well as the revelation needed to obtain salvation.[3]

A fourth reason we can trust the Bible's divine origin is its preservation. Some have called this the indestructibility of Scripture. The Bible has been the source of many censorship attempts to eradicate it from existence. In AD 303, Roman emperor Diocletian ordered all Bibles destroyed. A mere twenty years later, Constantine offered a reward for any remaining Bibles. Later, in 1199, Pope Innocent III ordered all Bibles burned and had anyone who tried to hide a copy placed under house arrest. In the 1920s, Joseph Stalin ordered all Bibles removed from the Soviet Union.

Regardless of the time in history, there have been attempts to destroy God's Word. Yet today the Bible stands as the world's most printed book. There are more copies in more languages than any other book in the world. It is available in nearly nine hundred languages in audio, and is available to anyone with an Internet connection in hundreds of languages. If every printed Bible were laid end to end, they would encircle the planet numerous times.

A fifth reason we can trust the Bible is found in its unique structure. As we have mentioned, it consists of sixty-six books written by approximately forty authors in three languages on three continents over about a 1,500-year period. Yet the individual books complement one another with amazing consistency. At the time each book was written, its human authors usually had no way of knowing what others would write, yet their words connect and reflect a consistent message, revealing God's divine words to humanity.

A sixth reason we can trust the Bible is from God is its universal influence. The Bible has impacted the world unlike any other document in history. It stands as the foundation book behind the laws of Western civilization, including many of the principles found in the U.S. Constitution. The Bible's accounts have inspired more songs, works of art, and other expressions than any other writing. From the music of Mozart and Handel to some of today's best inspirational music, the Bible's words continue to influence culture in untold ways.

A seventh reason we can trust the Bible is God's Word is found in its life-changing impact on the lives of people. No other work has divided and united nations while changing the souls of people. It is a matchless bestseller that appeals to the hearts and minds of people from every ethnic and economic background among every tribe and nation of the world.

Yet beyond its reach is its unmatched lasting impact. The testimonies of millions of men and women are profound evidence to support the Bible's influence. Many individuals, past and present, have experienced the truth of its promises, its wise counsel, and its inspiration in ways that have changed lives on earth and in eternity.

The Bible claims to be given by God to man. Its own testimony of itself and other lines of evidence, when taken together, make a strong case for the divine origin of the Bible and why we should trust it. All of these facts are best understood in terms of the Bible having a divine rather than merely human origin.

What About the Missing Books of the Bible?

This question relates to the subject of canonicity. When someone speaks of the "canon of Scripture," they are referring to the collection of the sixty-six recognized books that have come to be known as the Holy Bible. The word *canon* means "measuring rod." Christians believe that the Bible is the measuring stick God has given the human race for evaluation of what is true or false, right or wrong.

Just as a ruler helps the carpenter saw the board at precisely the correct length, our spiritual measuring instrument—the canon—helps us get things right according to what God wants for us.

But how did the volume of Scripture get compiled? Why did some ancient religious books from that era not make it in? For a variety of reasons, Christians accept that God determined canonicity. Over time, the people of God discovered which of these books were prophetic (and therefore canonical).

By the time of the early church, the inspired writings that would ultimately make up the New Testament began to achieve circulation. During this time, there were also writings in circulation that Christians recognized were not from God, and those were rejected for canonization.

Books from the Old and New Testament eras that were not recognized as belonging to the God-ordained collection of Scripture came to be known as "apocryphal" writings (meaning "hidden"). Origen (who lived AD 185–254) may have been the first scholar to use the word *apocryphal* in alerting early Christians to the questionable value of these non-inspired writings. Depending on how one divides the chapters or sections, there are a dozen apocryphal books that exist from the Old Testament era and about fifteen from the New Testament era.

The question becomes, Why should the apocryphal books be rejected as inspired (and therefore not part of the biblical canon)? Here are the answers: Unlike the actual biblical books, no apocryphal writing claims to have been penned by a prophet (in the case of the books from the Old Testament era) or can be shown as authored by one of Christ's original apostles (regarding writings from the New Testament era). Further, the New Testament quotes all Old Testament books but never quotes the apocryphal writings, except in one instance, Jude 9, which does not contradict the Old Testament. Also, Jesus never quoted from any of the apocryphal books.

Few early church leaders ever referenced the apocryphal writings the way they referenced canonical Scripture. Early church leaders who did not consider the Apocrypha to be canonical Scripture included Athanasius, Cyril of Jerusalem, Origen, and Jerome (a fourth-century biblical scholar and translator of the Latin Vulgate).

In the second century AD, the earliest copies of the Peshitta (the Syriac Bible) did not contain any of the apocryphal writings. When the Dead Sea Scrolls (a collection of more than nine hundred ancient texts) were discovered at a place called Qumran in the mid-1940s, included were commentaries on all of the Old Testament books. Some fragments of Jewish apocryphal writings were found, yet no written commentaries of these were present (as there were for all of the other Old Testament books).

One of the most respected Dead Sea Scroll scholars, Millar Burrows, said of these apocryphal writings, "There is no reason to think that any of these works were venerated as sacred Scripture."[4]

When considering questions about the apocryphal writings (and about canonicity in general), the comments and writings of notable leaders from the early Christian era are worth noting. Philo (who lived from 20 BC to AD 40) was a Jewish teacher from Egypt. He quoted the Old Testament prolifically, citing virtually every canonical book. However, he never once quoted from the Apocrypha as inspired.

Josephus (a Jewish historian who lived from AD 30 to 100) references the same thirty-nine books that we know as the Old Testament. Though demonstrating familiarity with them, he never quotes any apocryphal books as Scripture. The Westminster Confession of Faith (written in 1647) states: "The books commonly called Apocrypha, not being of divine inspiration, are not part of the canon of the Scriptures; and therefore are of no authority in the church of God, nor to be any otherwise approved, or made use of, than any other human writings."

In summary, we may be confident that the canon of Scripture is complete. Regarding the New Testament, Jesus alluded to the closing of the canon by the authority he appointed to his apostles, all of whom died before the end of the first century (see John 14:26; 15:27; 1 Corinthians 2:13).

How Can I Understand the Bible?

Even if we accept the Bible as God's inspired Word, it can still be difficult to understand. Where can we begin?

First, the best way to understand the Bible is to dive in and read it. Familiarity will grow into understanding with the Holy Spirit's help. Our faith needs the milk and meat of God's Word to be healthy and whole. Sometimes people avoid reading the Bible because it convicts them. The Bible is a shining light that exposes the deeds of the heart, whether good or evil. If you don't read the Bible, sin is more likely to creep in and erode your faith.

Second, several tools exist to help. In my book for parents, I offer six methods to study the Bible: studying the context, considering the manners and customs of the time period, finding out if a word or phrase has been used elsewhere in Scripture, looking up Greek and Hebrew terms and their meanings, examining figures of speech, and paying attention to the details of the passage.[5] There are also many tools to help in your study: study Bibles with explanatory notes, commentaries, Bible dictionaries, and more.

What About Apparent Bible Contradictions?

There are hundreds of websites that claim to list the "many contradictions" in the Bible. But the sites' arguments and so-called evidence of contradictions are nothing new, and upon closer examination aren't really contradictions.

First, ask, "What is the context?" For example, Matthew 7:21 says that not everyone who calls Jesus "Lord" will enter heaven. But Acts 2:21 says, "Everyone who calls on the name of the Lord will be saved." How do we deal with what appears to be a direct contradiction? The answer in this situation is found by looking closely at the context. In Matthew 7:21, Jesus was addressing how to recognize false teachers. They might claim to believe in Jesus but live in contrast with this claim. Jesus said these false teachers could be recognized by their "fruit" or actions.

In Acts 2:21, Peter was preaching to a large audience. When explaining to them how to become followers of Jesus, Peter taught they were to call on the name of the Lord, referring to Jesus. This is not a contradiction but rather two accounts in two different contexts.

Second, ask, "To whom was it written?" For example, in the Old Testament there are many rules about which foods are acceptable to eat and which foods are not. Yet in Romans 14:14 Paul wrote, "I am fully convinced that no food is unclean in itself." Isn't this a contradiction?

> "Having for many years made the evidences of Christianity the subject of close study, the result has been a firm and increasing conviction of the authenticity . . . of the Bible"
>
> Simon Greenleaf (1783–1853), professor, Harvard Law School

In the Old Testament, God gave the Jewish people many commands related to clean and unclean foods as part of the Law of Moses. After Jesus came to fulfill the Law, his followers were set free from these restrictions. Though some in the early church did not understand these changes at first, Paul wrote to clarify that these Jewish food laws were not necessary for those who were Christians. It is not a contradiction, but rather two passages written toward two different groups of people at different times.

Third, ask, "Are these passages complementary or contradictory?" Following the tragedy that took place at the World Trade Center on September 11, 2001, thousands of people lost their lives. Many witnesses experienced this scene and lived to tell about it. Each witness shares a different aspect of the event, yet they all speak about the same main event.

The same can be seen in the Bible, particularly in the four gospels, which include multiple accounts of the same events. We should expect each writer to include differences in details, though the same main events are taking place. For example, skeptics will sometimes point out that two demon-possessed men came toward Jesus in Matthew 8:28 while Mark and Luke both only mention one demon-possessed man. Isn't this a contradiction?

Not really. Both accounts share a consistent account yet offer variety in details. While Mark and Luke speak of one man Jesus freed from demons, Matthew chose to also mention another demon-possessed man who was at the same event. These stories complement one another, but they are not contradictions.

The birth accounts of Jesus are also often used in attempts to claim a Bible contradiction. Matthew included the visit of the wise men, while Luke left out the wise men but included the account of the shepherds who visited Jesus on the night he was born. Why didn't both Matthew and Luke include both accounts?

It is possible Matthew or Luke knew only one of the parts of this overall story of Christ's birth. Yet other possibilities exist. Perhaps Matthew wanted to emphasize the visit of the wise men to highlight Jesus as King of the Jews as part of his Jewish focus on Jesus. Perhaps Luke mentioned the shepherds due to emphasizing the involvement of angels as he did elsewhere in Luke and Acts. Regardless of the reasons, their accounts still do not contradict each other. The shepherds visited Jesus on the night he was born in a manger, while the wise men visited later when Jesus was in a house. There is no reason these two events should be seen as contradicting each other.

Upon his evaluation of hundreds of Bible contradictions, Old Testament scholar Gleason Archer noted:

As I have dealt with one apparent discrepancy after another and have studied the alleged contradictions between the biblical record and the evidence of linguistics, archaeology, or science, my confidence in the trustworthiness of Scripture has been repeatedly verified and strengthened by the discovery that almost every problem in Scripture that has ever been discovered by man, from ancient times until now, has been dealt with in a completely satisfactory manner by the biblical text itself—or else by objective archaeological information.[6]

The belief that the Bible is full of errors is a myth, yet one that continues to resonate with those who oppose its message. We would do well to focus on the evidence and seek the truth about God's Word and its implications for our lives.

Myth #9

Christianity can't be true because it is based on a dead man coming back to life

Truth: If the best explanation for the empty tomb of Jesus is the resurrection, then Christianity can be true

Have you ever seen a 1957 Chevrolet Bel Air? That's one hot car. Even back when I was a kid, the silhouette of a '57 Chevy with the bulging headlights and streamlined trunk fins on the back was already a part of American pop culture.

Jimmy Ellis, my sixteen-year-old neighbor, was sort of famous—and envied—in the neighborhood. He not only had a driver's license, but his first car was a '57 Chevy—a shiny, red, two-door Chevrolet Bel Air with a V-8 engine. Wherever he drove, it always drew a crowd. "Rev up the motor!" we'd yell. "Spin the tires!"

But Jimmy's Chevy wasn't always so hot. When I first saw the car, Jimmy was still a couple of years away from driving age. And at that point, the car hadn't seen a street or high school parking lot in a long time.

"Come with me," Jimmy said one afternoon as several of us were taking a break from playing tag football. "You can take a look at my car."

"You've got a car?" several of us asked in unison. He might as well have claimed to own a flying saucer. Car ownership was something we teen mortals could only dream of.

"Watch and learn," Jimmy told us.

We followed him through some woods, down a path, and then through some tall grass. I was about to conclude that this was some kind of joke when suddenly there it was, surrounded by briars and covered with more rust than paint. Underneath what looked like a hundred years of neglect was the unmistakable outline of a 1957 Chevy Bel Air.

For a few minutes, our small group of teen guys just stood around, looking over the car. So much potential, but so much to fix! Could the engine ever run again? *How will they ever get this thing out of the woods?* I wondered.

Jimmy broke the reverent silence. "This 1957 Chevy is going to be awesome!" he announced. "My dad and I are gonna give this car a complete restoration."

"A restoration? What's that?" someone asked. Jimmy looked each of us directly in the eye. "It means that my dad is going to bring this car back from the dead."

Back From the Dead

As great as the restoration of a classic car is, a resurrection of a lifeless human body is more impressive. The resurrection of

Jesus Christ changed history—and eternity—for every human who has ever lived.

When it comes to the truths of Christianity, and specifically to the issue of Christ's physical resurrection from death, we have strong evidence. What makes Christianity a unique belief system? It is the fact that our founder, leader, and Lord had the power to bring himself back to life. Jesus Christ beat death, and did so for us as well.

People understand the concept of restoration. We restore antique furniture, 1957 Chevy's, and Victorian houses. In a restoration, broken things get fixed and obsolete parts get updated. It entails bringing something back to its original condition. The Christian concept of resurrection goes further. The New Testament resurrection of Christ depicts Jesus as not only alive, but glorified. It was more than the mere reanimation of a corpse.

> "Even if the disciples had believed in Jesus' resurrection, it is doubtful they would have generated any following. So long as the body was interred in the tomb, a Christian movement founded on belief in the resurrection of the dead man would have been an impossible folly."
>
> William Lane Craig, PhD

Resurrection is a crucial component of our faith. And while mystery cults and world religions allude to it, only Christianity has history on its side. The biblical worldview is unparalleled in its promise of a resurrected body for the believer, and Christianity is certainly distinct in that its founder alone—Jesus Christ—could and did enact his own resurrection. Jesus' return after three days in the tomb is a vital, nonnegotiable point of doctrine, because Jesus said before going to the cross that his resurrection would prove he was the Savior (Matthew 12:39–40; Romans 1:4).

Both Christians and non-Christians may wonder how we can know for certain that Jesus rose from the dead. But we need to ask an even more fundamental question first.

Did Jesus Really Exist?

Many skeptics want to know if there is historical evidence for Jesus other than that found in the New Testament. Actually, the New Testament records of Jesus should be allowed as corroborative evidence for Jesus. The New Testament accounts of Jesus Christ meet a number of key criteria by which scholars determine if something is historically trustworthy: The New Testament record comes to us from eyewitness sources and was written close to the time of events recorded.

Furthermore, the New Testament provides consistent content that harmonizes with other known facts about Jesus, and biblical accounts were universally affirmed by contemporaries who were in the know. Had the New Testament gotten it wrong about Jesus, there were eyewitnesses living at the time of the writings who could have set the record straight.

Not only did none of the early church leaders refute what the New Testament said about Jesus, but many of them also died for the message of Jesus. Quite literally, apostles (those who had seen the risen Christ) such as Peter and Paul, plus the next generation of Christian leaders (such as Polycarp and Chrysostom), laid down their lives for the veracity of what the New Testament recorded. All of these realities taken together make a strong case for the Gospels' trustworthiness as historical sources.

Rudolf Bultmann—a German scholar whose approach of "demythologizing" Jesus called on people in the twentieth century to focus more on faith than on historical facts—made the following observation:

> Of course the doubt as to whether Jesus really existed is unfounded and not worth refutation. No sane person can doubt that Jesus stands as the founder behind the historical movement whose first distinct stage is represented by the oldest Palestinian community.[1]

In other words, Jesus did exist, and what those first Christians reported about him can be trusted as factual.

Even if we set the New Testament records of Jesus aside, an impressive amount of historical testimony about him comes to us from the ancient world. This includes secular source material such as that from Tacitus, a first-century Roman historian. Tacitus records that Christ suffered under Pontius Pilate during the reign of Tiberius. Suetonius—another Roman historian and chief secretary to Emperor Hadrian—recorded that one named Chrestus (or Christ) lived during the first century. Julius Africanus (who lived in the second century) quotes Thallus (a Samaritan whose writings are from about twenty years after Christ's death), who documented the darkness that followed the crucifixion. Julius Africanus was a famous orator who appears to have assumed as factual what Thallus had said about Jesus.

> "I claim to be an historian. My approach to Classics is historical. And I tell you that the evidence for the life, the death, and the resurrection of Christ is better authenticated than most of the facts of ancient history."
>
> E. M. Blaiklock (1903–1983), classics chair, Auckland University, New Zealand

Other secular sources that reference Jesus, and whose testimony corroborates what the New Testament says about him, include Pliny the Younger (Roman lawyer and political figure born about AD 61), Lucian of Samosata (a Greek humorist born about AD 125 and known for his sarcasm), and Mara Bar-Serapion (a Syrian writer, living near the end of the first century).

Another later (though important) source is the Babylonian Talmud (Jewish writings compiled during the third century). Contained therein is a reference to Jesus, who gave Israel new teachings and was executed at Passover for this.

The bottom line is that from sources other than the New Testament (and note that these are non-Christian sources), we may conclude many of the same things that the Gospels tell us about Jesus. Historians accept as genuine other persons and events with much less supporting evidence, so we can reasonably accept that what we know of Jesus Christ is historically reliable. It is highly significant that during the first three hundred years of Christianity (a time of intense persecution), thousands of followers were so convinced of the reality of Jesus that they were willing to die for him.

An Atheist Teacher

My first exposure to an atheist came in my tenth grade biology class. We were starting a unit on evolution, and although I was not a Christian at the time, it was not hard to see that Darwin's theory left little need for God. The teacher was a very militant and outspoken unbeliever. I am sure that today no high school teacher would be able to do what I am about to relate without some disciplinary action. But back in 1981 rules and protocols weren't as clearly defined as today.

With utmost sarcasm the teacher explained that we were learning about science, and science has nothing to do with God or religion. The teacher forcefully said, "Don't be bringing any Bible booklets to me, and don't tell me that Charles Darwin had some deathbed conversion. He didn't. That legend is absolutely false." He explained that evolution was a proven fact, and while going to church and belief in God are fine in the privacy of our spare time, his classroom would not be open to those things. "I don't want any parents calling me and trying to convert me," he commanded.

Now this teacher had a pointer that he used which was very much like a long wooden dowel. As he talked he would frequently tap on his desk when he wasn't pointing to words on the blackboard. I guess his disclaimer about evolution and his warning to all the possible creationists in the room got his adrenaline pumping that day, because one of the raps of the wooden pointer on the desk caused it to break. Frustrated, the teacher threw the broken pieces in a nearby wastebasket.

To everyone's surprise he then reached above the blackboard and pulled a small American flag out of a little bracket that held it to the wall. I'm sure that you have seen this kind of flag—it was probably fourteen inches long on a wooden stick similar to the pointer that had just broken. For all I know, this flag had presided over the classroom for decades. Grabbing the stick, the teacher ripped the cloth flag off, leaving a couple of little staples behind. He wadded up the flag, tossed it in the trashcan, pointed to the blackboard, and resumed his presentation on Darwin. The class sat in shocked silence. Sensing the awkwardness of the moment, the teacher turned around, looked at all of us, and said, "What?" With near anger in his voice he said, "You people need to chill out."

That was my first exposure to atheism, and it was a moment I will never forget. Now, many years later, I know that not all atheists are angry, unpatriotic, or crusading to steal away the faith of teenagers, but many are. For weeks my fellow students and I talked about that encounter. I began to try to formulate an understanding of this even though it would be five more years before I personally became a Christian.

Three things are worth pointing out: First, I was not a confident defender of the faith at that point and in fact not even a Christian yet, and I don't want young people to feel like they have failed if they can't defend God or creation the first time they ever encounter an atheist. To understand the dozens and dozens of attacks that come to Christianity takes much study and consistent commitment. Fortunately, you will grow as a believer while you prepare to help others through their spiritual objections. Just be willing to start where you are and nurture your walk and witness.

Second, this encounter convinced me that behind unbelief is often some sort of pain. I believe that those who reject God—especially those with an "angry" unbelief like my biology teacher—have some sort of emotional pain in their background. For this reason, patience and kindness must be exhibited even while not compromising the truth of the gospel.

Third and finally, this encounter was one thing God used to set me on the path that would ultimately lead me to my own conversion. I reasoned that if God exists he would certainly be powerful enough to create the world. If God were powerful enough to create the solar system and planet Earth, I figured he would be powerful enough to create the human race. And if God could create people and all of these other things, I concluded that he could do anything, even raise the dead. By my freshman year in college, though I still had not personally committed my life to Christ, I had come to believe that God must be real and there was no logical reason to reject his ability to act in this world. I figured, why not? If there is a God, why couldn't he part the Red Sea? Why couldn't he feed the 5,000? If you can call a universe into existence, even resurrection of a dead body should be no problem.

Views Regarding the Resurrection

And speaking of Christ's resurrection, it is worth pointing out that many view this as the crowning proof of Christianity. I agree. If Jesus really rose from the grave, the Christian faith is established. It's fact. Reality. This news is really good, and this message is really true.

The disciples preached that the empty tomb was proof of Christ and salvation, and this message was for all people. The apostles were people who had seen the risen Jesus—or at least they claimed to, so let's look at the options here.

If Jesus hadn't risen, but his followers told people that he did, and they knew he hadn't, they were liars. If they thought he had risen, but he hadn't, and they were unaware that he hadn't, they were mistaken. If Jesus didn't rise, but the disciples had some sort of hallucination or imaginary vision, then they were spreading a false report without realizing it. Many variations of these possibilities have been suggested.

But here are some facts of history that even non-Christian scholars acknowledge: After Jesus' crucifixion, the tomb was discovered to be empty, and different people at different times and different places began to report having seen the risen Jesus. There was also an instantaneous change in the lives of the disciples. Not only did formerly frightened, discouraged followers begin to bravely proclaim that Jesus was alive, in fact thousands of pious Jews began to worship on Sunday within a few decades. This point alone is monumental when you remember that the people of Israel had kept a Saturday Sabbath for centuries and their relationship with God depended on this. Why suddenly would huge segments begin to worship on Sunday? Because that was resurrection day. Let's not forget the changed lives of James and Saul. James (a brother of Jesus) had initially doubted. James was likely one of the family members who initially viewed Jesus' claims as Messiah to be incredible (see Mark 3:21). Saul of Tarsus had been an unrelenting opponent of Christianity, yet would radically turn to become one of its greatest evangelists. He would even go on to write more than half of the New Testament.

These are facts that even "critical scholars" do not dispute. Regarding the hundreds of early Christians who claimed to experience and encounter the risen Jesus (see 1 Corinthians 15), what we know about their lives is simply exemplary. Those who saw the risen Jesus, proclaimed the message, and then were willing to die for their faith exhibited no signs of dishonesty, malice, or delusions. They weren't liars and they weren't crazy. The conclusion in light of all the known facts is that Jesus really did rise.

Do the Resurrection Accounts Conflict?

Skeptics often argue that the resurrection accounts somehow conflict. However, if the resurrection accounts presented in the four gospels were in seamless agreement, skeptics would probably accuse the early church of having engaged in some sort of conspiracy. If the police hear the exact same story from witnesses, for example, they become suspicious. It means the witnesses probably got together and made it up.

The unique attributes of each gospel account actually contribute to the overall authenticity of testimony for Jesus' resurrection. On the surface there may seem to be discrepancies, but there are no actual contradictions. The truth is that no single account of the resurrection completely exhausts the event. Just as different eyewitnesses to an accident will give varying testimonies, all of which are true, the "reporters" of the resurrection chose to include the details that were important to them. There is a basic order given in all of the resurrection accounts that when studied removes the apparent contradictions.

A detailed look at the appearances of Jesus is as follows:

Appearance #1

The first Jesus sighting occurred early Sunday morning: "When Jesus rose early on the first day of the week, he appeared first to Mary Magdalene, out of whom he had driven seven demons" (Mark 16:9).

The full story reveals that Mary's first reaction was grief. This is understandable for someone who had lost a loved one. When she saw a person near the tomb, she thought it was a gardener, not Jesus. It was only when Jesus spoke to her that she recognized his voice. She clung to him and then ran to tell the others (John 20:11–18).

Does anything in this story seem out of place? Only a dead man who is alive. That's the point. Jesus alive is the one supernatural, stunning highlight of the account.

Appearance #2

As Mary Magdalene and "the other Mary" returned from the tomb, we read in Matthew 28:9–10, "Suddenly Jesus met them. 'Greetings,' he said. They came to him, clasped his feet and worshiped him. Then Jesus said to them, 'Do not be afraid. Go and tell my brothers to go to Galilee; there they will see me.'"

Here we find two women who saw the risen Jesus. Other women are mentioned in Luke (Mary Magdalene, Joanna, Mary the mother of James, and "the others"). Several women must have been present. This was significant in Jewish culture because all matters required two or three witnesses to be confirmed as a fact. Their response? They returned to the disciples to tell the amazing news. Again, this reaction is normal with the exception that Jesus was spotted alive.

Appearance #3

As two men traveled the road from Jerusalem to Emmaus, Jesus began walking with them, asking questions and sharing his interpretations of the Jewish prophecies regarding the Messiah. They later stop to share a meal together. When they do, they then realize it is Jesus (Mark 16:12–13; Luke 24:13–31).

Appearance #4

Continuing the story above, the two Emmaus walkers returned to Jerusalem to find the disciples. "There they found the

Eleven and those with them, assembled together and saying, 'It is true! The Lord has risen and has appeared to Simon'" (Luke 24:33–34). Apparently somewhere between the time Jesus disappeared from dinner to the time these two men relayed their story to the eleven disciples, Jesus had appeared to Peter (who was also known as Simon).

Paul notes this again in 1 Corinthians 15:4–5: "[Jesus] was raised on the third day according to the Scriptures, and that he appeared to Cephas [Peter]." Peter would later stand in the streets of Jerusalem on the crowded holiday of Pentecost to call thousands to follow this risen Jesus. By this point, we have four sightings by several people—at least four women and three men—all before nightfall on the Sunday of Jesus' resurrection.

Appearance #5

The next appearance was to ten of the disciples, the two men returning from Emmaus, and probably the women and perhaps additional followers. Instead of seven people encountering a resurrected Jesus, we now have at least a dozen men plus women and any others in the room (Luke 24:36–43; John 20:19–23).

First, they were scared and thought they had seen a ghost. They saw his hands and feet but still did not believe what they were experiencing. Jesus then eats food in their midst, and they finally realize this Jesus before them is not a spirit but a real resurrected body!

Appearance #6

For an entire week, Thomas must have wrestled with the arguments of over a dozen people, including his closest friends, who attempted to convince him that Jesus was really alive.

A week later his disciples were in the house again, and Thomas was with them. Though the doors were locked, Jesus came and

154

stood among them and said, "Peace be with you!" Then he said to Thomas, "Put your finger here; see my hands. Reach out your hand and put it into my side. Stop doubting and believe."

Thomas said to him, "My Lord and my God!"

John 20:26–28

Appearance #7

Jesus' seventh sighting interestingly took place with seven of his disciples. In John 21, we find that over half of the remaining disciples had taken an all-night fishing trip on the Sea of Galilee. This would not have really been out of the ordinary since many of these men were fishermen by trade and would have likely needed some food or fish to exchange for other goods during this intense period of time together in Jerusalem. The unordinary part was the guy standing on the shore in the morning:

Early in the morning, Jesus stood on the shore, but the disciples did not realize that it was Jesus. He called out to them, "Friends, haven't you any fish?"

"No," they answered.

He said, "Throw your net on the right side of the boat and you will find some." When they did, they were unable to haul the net in because of the large number of fish.

Then the disciple whom Jesus loved said to Peter, "It is the Lord!"

John 21:4–7

Appearance #8

Paul later writes that over five hundred people saw the resurrected Jesus at one time: "After that, he appeared to more than five hundred of the brothers and sisters at the same time, most of whom are still living, though some have fallen asleep" (1 Corinthians 15:6).

Why was this of great significance? It makes the issue much broader than Jesus' core group of followers. If only the original friends of Jesus said he was alive, it would be much easier to dismiss them. But with *hundreds* of verifiable witnesses, how could anyone reading Paul's letter not seriously consider that Jesus was really alive?

Appearance #9

In the same chapter, Paul tells us, "Then he appeared to James" (v. 7). James was known as the brother of Jesus, leader of the Jerusalem church, and author of the New Testament book of James. Prior to this experience with the risen Jesus, he was portrayed as skeptical of his brother's actions (John 17:5). However, after this encounter with the resurrected Jesus, he is seen as a proponent and leader of the early Christian movement.

Appearance #10

Once again the eleven disciples spotted Jesus, this time on a mountain in Galilee: "Then the eleven disciples went to Galilee, to the mountain where Jesus had told them to go. When they saw him, they worshiped him" (Matthew 28:16–17).

This sighting leaves us with the purpose Jesus charged to his followers: "Go and make disciples of all nations, baptizing them in the name of the Father and of the Son and of the Holy Spirit, and teaching them to obey everything I have commanded you" (Matthew 28:19–20).

Appearance #11

The final Jesus sighting by the core group of disciples occurred just before Jesus flew back to heaven: "When he had led them out to the vicinity of Bethany, he lifted up his hands and blessed them. While he was blessing them, he left them and was

156

taken up into heaven. Then they worshiped him and returned to Jerusalem with great joy. And they stayed continually at the temple, praising God" (Luke 24:50–53).

Appearance #12

A couple of years later, Saul was arresting those who followed Jesus. He even stood by in approval of Stephen's death as the first Christian martyr. But in Acts 9, Luke recorded that Saul physically saw Jesus while walking to Damascus. Soon baptized as a Christian, he became known as Paul and began Christianity's major expansions throughout the Roman Empire.

We can have confidence Jesus existed, died, and resurrected as the Gospels declare. As the Nicene Creed states, "he was crucified under Pontius Pilate; he suffered death and was buried. On the third day he rose again . . . he ascended into heaven and is seated at the right hand of the Father. He will come again in glory to judge the living and the dead."

Myth #10

Christianity isn't real because a loving God wouldn't send anyone to hell

Truth: God has made great efforts to make sure many will spend eternity with him

Could a loving God really send anyone to hell? Many people, including Christians, wrestle with this issue. In 2011, popular pastor Rob Bell published a *New York Times* bestselling book titled *Love Wins*, which questioned this very notion. While his own personal views appeared to never be clear, he presented significant doubts about the Bible's traditional view of hell. In his preface, he writes,

> A staggering number of people have been taught that a select few Christians will spend forever in a peaceful, joyous place called heaven, while the rest of humanity spends forever in torment and punishment in hell with no chance for anything better. . . . This

is misguided and toxic and ultimately subverts the contagious spread of Jesus's message of love, peace, forgiveness, and joy that our world desperately needs to hear.[1]

Would God really send the billions of non-Christians around the world to a place of eternal punishment and pain? How could a God who exhibits perfect love be reconciled with such a dreadful attitude of judgment?

In this chapter, we'll take a look at this important controversy. We'll address the reality of future judgment, how this judgment can coexist with a loving God, and why this understanding is vital for our lives and the lives of others today.

What Happens After We Die?

Many views have been offered regarding what happens to us after death. These common views include:

- **Atheism:** This life is all there is. There is nothing after death.
- **Reincarnation:** People return to life on earth in various forms with some systems, including an eventual achievement of enlightenment or oneness with the universe.
- **Universalism:** Everyone goes to heaven or paradise after death.
- **Annihilationism:** Some people go to heaven and all others are annihilated or cease to exist. Hell does not exist or at least does not exist forever.
- **Purgatory:** Heaven and hell exist, along with a temporary state in which people must be cleansed of sins before reaching heaven.
- **Soul Sleep:** The souls of dead believers "sleep" until the final judgment, and then go to heaven.

- **Heaven and Hell:** This traditional biblical concept teaches that there are only two options following death: eternal life in heaven for the follower of God and an eternal hell for those apart from him.

With so many options, it is easy to understand why people are often confused about whether hell exists or what happens after this life.

Is Hell Real?

While most people would like to believe heaven is real, few people want to accept that hell is a literal place where people would suffer for eternity. Some people even seek to rewrite the definition of hell by reinterpreting Scripture. The most common passage used to support this view is Matthew 5:22. The word used for *hell* in this verse is *Gehenna*, from a Greek form of the Hebrew word that means "Valley of Hinnom."[2]

This valley ran outside the walls of Jerusalem and was used in Old Testament times for human sacrifices to the pagan god Molech. King Josiah put a stop to this dreadful practice (2 Kings 23:10), and the Valley of Hinnom came to be used as a place where human excrement and rubbish were disposed of and burned. It was, in effect, a giant trash dump. The fire of *Gehenna* never went out, and the worms never died, so it came to be used symbolically of the place of divine punishment.

Annihilationists focus on the idea that what goes there is burned up. Edward W. Fudge, one of the main proponents of this view, holds that this idea means the fires destroy completely. But he "appears to underinterpret *Gehenna*. He does this in part by committing the exegetical fallacy of confusing referent (the Valley of Hinnom outside of Jerusalem and the mundane burning that allegedly occurred there) and sense (a place of extraordinary punishment prepared by God for his enemies). . . . the latter [is what] Jesus warns against; the connotative meaning (sense) of Matthew 5:22 is primarily God's hell, not a Judean waste disposal site."[3] In short, Jesus used the idea of *Gehenna* as an image so his audience could sense the reality of hell.

Annihilationists also cite Matthew 5:29–30. They consider the whole body going to hell to mean a complete loss of one's person or identity. They view it as a complete destruction of a person's body and soul. But being thrown into hell is "active punishment, not a 'passive loss.'"[4]

Hell is presented as an eternal, conscious punishment in Scripture. This leads some to object that hell is the greatest of all evils. How could God, who is all loving, send people to a place like hell? The answer is ultimately in the juxtaposition of justice and love seen most clearly at the cross. How can God be both loving and forgiving and yet just and punish sin? The answer is Jesus. He sent his Son to pay the price of sin so that justice can be served and people can receive forgiveness.

> "God sends no one to hell. We send ourselves. God has done all that is necessary for us to be forgiven, redeemed, cleansed and made fit for heaven. All that remains is for us to receive this gift."
>
> Paul Little, *Know Why You Believe*

To be just, God must punish sin; he cannot let evil reign (Romans 6:23). Those who sin must pay the price, which is death. Death here is referring to hell. This is not just a physical death; it is a spiritual death. Those who do not choose Christ are separated from him for all eternity. But his love is also seen in that he does not annihilate those who do not choose him, for that would go against his nature. He cannot destroy the soul, which is good. But he can banish what is evil. He allows the one who does not choose him to have what he or she wanted, that is, separation from him forever. They did not desire his presence, and so he allows them to be forever removed from him.

A Look at Lazarus

An important passage related to the reality of hell is given by Jesus in Luke 16:19–31. In this account, he speaks about an unnamed rich man and a poor man named Lazarus who both die. Immediately following their deaths, Jesus says regarding Lazarus, "The angels carried him to Abraham's side" (v. 22). In contrast, the rich man is "in Hades, where he was in torment" (v. 23). Interestingly, the rich man can see Abraham and Lazarus in the distance (v. 23).

The rich man first asks for water to cool his torment, but Abraham replies that "a great chasm has been set in place, so that those who want to go from here to you cannot, nor can anyone cross over from there to us" (v. 26). Meanwhile, Lazarus lives in comfort (v. 25).

The rich man then begs for someone to reach his family to keep them from the pain of hell. To this, Abraham replies that they have Moses and the Prophets (v. 29). The passage ends with the rich man asking for someone from the dead to speak to his family, to which Abraham replies, "If they do not listen to Moses and the Prophets, they will not be convinced even if someone rises from the dead" (v. 31).

Many insights can be observed from Jesus' teaching in this passage. **First, heaven and hell are real places.** This is not called a parable, but refers to a real person—Abraham—and a real situation—the afterlife of two people and what takes place there.

Second, entrance into heaven or hell is immediate. Lazarus is at "Abraham's side," a descriptive way of saying he is with God. If any Jew were in heaven, it would have been Abraham. Using this person would have strongly resonated with the original audience listening to this teaching. Likewise, entrance into hell is immediate.

Third, heaven is a place of comfort while hell is a place of torment. Verse 23 calls Hades "torment," while in verse 24 the rich man calls it "agony in this fire."

Fourth, residence in heaven or hell is permanent. There is no way to move from hell to heaven. Abraham says, "Between us and you a great chasm has been set in place, so that those who want to go from here to you cannot, nor can anyone cross over from there to us" (v. 26).

Fifth, heaven and hell are the only options in the afterlife. There is no mention of purgatory in this account, nor is this concept mentioned at all in the Bible. This concept has a long history, especially in the Roman Catholic tradition, but is not based on the Bible's teachings.

Sixth, the decisions we make in this life determine where we will spend eternal life. There is no "return to go," reincarnation, or second chance after this life. Hebrews 9:27 teaches, "People are destined to die once, and after that to face judgment." We are called to believe in Christ now, and to share him with others who have yet to believe.

Seventh, not everyone will be in heaven. On the positive side, Revelation 5:9 notes, "You are worthy to take the scroll and to open its seals, because you were slain, and with your blood you purchased for God persons from every tribe and language and people and nation." People from every place around the earth will be in heaven. Revelation 7:9 also mentions, "After this I looked, and there before me was a great multitude that no one could count, from every nation, tribe, people and language, standing before the throne and before the Lamb." Yet despite the great number of people in heaven from every part of the earth, not everyone will live there. Many will also endure the agony and torment of hell apart from the Lord.

Universalists Beware

It has become increasingly popular to suggest that everyone goes to heaven, except maybe a few really bad people. Even some

Christians claim everyone will eventually make it to heaven. This error highlights the variations of universalism that exist today. These include:

- **Traditional or Radical Universalism:** Everyone goes to heaven following death.
- **Evangelical Universalism:** Everyone who believes in some form of God will be saved.
- **Eventual Universalism:** Everyone will eventually make it to heaven, either after purgatory or in the end when God makes all things new.

One Bible passage commonly cited by universalists as supporting their beliefs is 1 Timothy 2:3–4: "This is good, and pleases God our Savior, who wants all people to be saved and to come to a knowledge of the truth." But this passage doesn't explicitly say that God *will* save everyone, only that he "wants" all to come to know the truth. By his very nature, the loving God must desire everyone to be saved, but this does not mean that everyone *will* be saved, especially in light of biblical evidence to the contrary.

Though popular, these ideas are actually spiritually dangerous. To claim everyone will make it to heaven, will make it through any belief in any god, or will eventually make it to heaven removes the responsibility of people to respond to the salvation offered through Jesus Christ. Worse, it eliminates the need for holy living as well as the motivation to take the gospel to those who have yet to hear.

What About Those Who Haven't Heard the Gospel?

The Scriptures are clear that those who believe in Jesus will be saved (John 1:12). But what about those who have never heard

> "For since the creation of the world God's invisible qualities—his eternal power and divine nature—have been clearly seen, being understood from what has been made, so that people are without excuse."
>
> Romans 1:20

about Jesus? Millions of people have never heard about Jesus *at all*. Will God still condemn them to hell? As one student asked me on a college campus, "Do you mean God is going to send some people to hell simply because they haven't heard the name of Jesus? Would a person be lost because their only crime is being born on the wrong continent?"

This again is one of the main concerns highlighted in Rob Bell's *Love Wins*. He writes,

> Of all the billions of people who have ever lived, will only a select number "make it to a better place" and every single other person suffer in torment and punishment forever? Is this acceptable to God? . . . Does God punish people for thousands of years with infinite, eternal torment for things they did in their few finite years of life? This doesn't just raise disturbing questions about God; it raises questions about the beliefs themselves. . . . If there are only a select few who go to heaven, which is more terrifying to fathom: the billions who burn forever or the few who escape this fate? . . . What kind of faith is that? Or, more important: what kind of God is that?[5]

God has not forgotten the unreached people of this world. First Timothy 2:4 clearly states that God "wants all people to be saved and to come to a knowledge of the truth." Acts 17:26–27 teaches that God has determined the times and places for everyone to live "so that they would seek him and perhaps reach out for him and find him, though he is not far from any one of us."

Scripture and contemporary missionary evidence support the claim that those who seek God based on the light they have will be given the knowledge of the gospel in some way, even if part or all of the process happens supernaturally (as was the case for Cornelius in Acts 10). This view satisfies the claim that a loving God would make salvation universally available, but it avoids the problematic claims of universalism and of inclusivism that people can be saved without knowledge of the gospel.

A striking example from modern missions in support of this position is told by Don Richardson in the book *Eternity in Their Hearts*. A man named Warrasa Wange from the Gedeo people of Ethiopia cried out to "Magano" (his tribe's notion of the highest and most benevolent deity). Warrasa asked the deity to reveal himself. Almost immediately, Warrassa began having visions of two white men building shelters under a large tree in his village. A voice in the visions told him, "These men will bring you a message from Magano, the God you seek. Wait for them." Eight years later, two Canadian missionaries came to Warrasa's village and met him under the same tree he saw in his vision. The missionaries shared the gospel, and Warrasa and many of his fellow tribesmen believed.[6]

I believe this is a compelling example of God getting the gospel to a person who honestly sought him based on the light he had. But his salvation was based on the gospel he came to believe, not just on the light he had initially.

A few years ago, I met a man from Papua New Guinea who grew up as an aborigine and had never heard the name of God or Jesus. Yet even as a young boy, he would look to the sky and pray, "God, I want to know you." Was he praying specifically to the God of the Bible? Did he know the Gospel? Not at that time. But he was aware of his need and would try to appease the gods by cutting himself. His tribe believed that there were spirits alive in the forest. In an act of sacrifice, he would gouge his arms, thinking that the more pain he brought on himself, the more pleased these gods would be.

"Even as I did that, I knew it wasn't right," he told me. "I wanted to know the true God. I knew there had to be a real God beyond the gods in the trees." Years later he heard of some Christian missionaries visiting the area and traveled to see them. As soon as they told him about Jesus, he knew this was the one true God he had been waiting to meet.

On a different occasion I traveled to Shabwalala, a small, dusty town one hundred miles outside of the capital of Zambia. As I stood in a field talking with a group of African boys, we heard a clanging noise slowly coming down the nearby path. I turned to see a thin cow with a bell around its neck. An old man was leading it down the road with a tattered rope. The man immediately came up to me and began talking to my translator, Abel Tembo.

"This man walked a day and a half to meet with you," Abel translated. "He heard there were white missionaries from America visiting, and he has a question he wants to ask you." When I asked Abel about the cow, he said the man couldn't leave his only cow behind or it would be stolen. As Abel told me this, the man began to point up at the sky and all around him while rattling off unfamiliar words.

"I know there is a god," he said to me through Abel, "because all of this had to come from somewhere. It couldn't have come from nothing. But I don't know where to take it from there."

I was emotionally moved. Here stood a man near the end of his life, weathered by trials and storms. He clearly had little to eat, yet there was a burning desire inside him to leave everything for the chance to meet someone who could introduce him to God.

It was only a short conversation before he accepted Jesus into his heart. "I have sought this my whole life," he said with tears in his eyes, his life changed forever and the weight of the world lifted off his shoulders. He asked if I would come to his village. "There are thirteen more who need to know this," he pleaded. We went and saw thirteen more souls added to the kingdom of God.

Unresolved Mysteries

God continues to reach the unreached in powerful ways, yet even these blessings do not answer every situation. The Bible does not clearly teach what will happen to those who never receive the Good News of the Gospel but do attempt to seek God. As C. S. Lewis puts it in *Mere Christianity*, "The truth is God has not told us what His arrangements about the other people are."[7] The best we can do is to trust in God's wisdom, mercy, and grace, and to suspend judgment as to the salvation of the unreached.

In reality, there is only one person of whom you may speak authoritatively regarding the condition of the soul: yourself. The bottom line is that we can trust that God, who loves the whole world, will take care of the questionable situations.

Yet the tension still lies in the timeless truth that "salvation is found in no one else [but Jesus], for there is no other name under heaven given to men by which we must be saved" (Acts 4:12). The real issue isn't that God sends people to hell because they lived in the wrong place at the wrong time and never heard about Jesus. The issue is that everyone knows the truth on some level, but many choose to "suppress" it (Romans 1:18).

> "There are only two kinds of people in the end: those who say to God, 'Thy will be done,' and those to whom God says, in the end, 'Thy will be done.'"
>
> Professor/scholar/author
> C. S. Lewis (1898–1963)

God's perfect nature assures us that he will always do the right thing (Genesis 18:25). He's beyond fair; he's rich in mercy and love (Ephesians 2:4). When we truly seek him, God promises we will find him: "You will seek me and find me when you seek me with all your heart" (Jeremiah 29:13).

Could It Really Be True?

Could it really be true that the key to heaven is having a relationship with Jesus Christ? To our twenty-first-century ears, this sounds really exclusive and very narrow. We don't like to be told, "You have only one option." But the question about reality is not, "Do I like it?" but rather, "Is this how things really are? Is this true?"

Regarding Jesus as the one and only way of salvation, let's use our imaginations for a moment. Just imagine, "What if it really is true? What if Jesus really did rise from the grave?" If he did, wouldn't it be reasonable to believe his claim to be God and the one means of redemption? Ask yourself, "Is this intrinsically possible? Is it possible that Jesus is the one and only Savior?"

The answer is yes. It is possible. Christianity is not like believing in square circles or a four-sided triangle. Those things are intrinsically impossible. Regarding Jesus being the only one who can grant eternal life, you may not yet believe that it is actual, but it is possible. We engage in exclusivities all the time: If you have lung cancer, putting a cast on your ankle will not help. Specific illnesses must be treated with specific medicines or procedures. If you are in Raleigh, North Carolina, and want to drive to Washington, D.C., I-40 west will not get you there. You must get on I-95 north. And just as not any road will take you to our nation's capital, arriving in heaven depends on taking the right road. What makes Jesus different is that while he did make exclusivist claims, he coupled his statements with unparalleled types of confirming proof.

Perhaps you would say, "I am a spiritual person already, and I'm comfortable with my doubts. Why do you insist that people see God from your perspective?" Rather than speak about God in specific terms, many prefer to handle the ultimate questions of this life (and the next) in terms of vague generalities. In C. S. Lewis's *Screwtape Letters*, the apprentice demon is encouraged to deceive people in this way: "Keep his mind off the plain antithesis between True and False."[8] In other words, a potent way to keep people from the truth of the gospel is to lull them into assuming that there is no actual truth to embrace or error to avoid. There are only feelings and opinions—mine, yours, and everybody else's—with none being more or less correct than any other.

C. S. Lewis asserts that such "spirituality" is the oldest heresy in Christian history because it denies devils and denies sin. What do you believe? Are you denying the reality of sin and the devil? Do you think there is a difference between spirituality and religion? While it may feel good to think of ourselves as spiritual, this means little without specific definitions based on objective reality.

More and more Americans say that religious beliefs have no influence on their lives. Into this context, Christianity offers objective, testable truth claims, corroborated by evidence that may be investigated.

The question is, What will you do with Christ? I challenge you to investigate the evidence and give God a chance to prove himself to you. It will change your life forever.

Final Thoughts

The church lobby was crowded with people filing out of the sanctuary where I had just given a talk on apologetics. During the course of my presentation on Christianity and skepticism, I had explained that one common profile represents what I call, "the wounded skeptic." I met "Robert," who had an inspiring journey about moving from a heart of wounded unbelief to having a vibrant faith in Jesus. Before relating his story, let me explain about what I believe is the most common profile of skepticism.

A "wounded skeptic" is someone whose aversion to God originated through painful life events. I have talked with many wounded skeptics. For a variety of projects, it has been my privilege to interview numerous atheists and agnostics (including well-known atheist leaders Michael Shermer, David Silverman, and the late Christopher Hitchens, to name a few). The insights gleaned about skepticism and the mind-set of the unbeliever are, I feel, fascinating. Learning why a given individual turns away from God—and then may become obsessively hostile toward God—can be a riveting (and often poignant) study. When a person can process their pain in a way that results in a turning *to* God rather than *against* him, ultimately arriving at a place of trust in and relationship with Christ, it is a beautiful thing. Robert's story is one such inspiring tale.

It was a beautiful spring Sunday morning in Pennsylvania when the line at my book table brought Robert before me. Smiling and enthusiastic, this man in his mid-fifties said some very complimentary things about my sermon. "I was one of those wounded skeptics," he said. "And what you described is exactly where my heart and mind once were."

Robert and his wife told me about their business, their involvement in their church, and how much they enjoyed helping others. Robert told me about a 5K run he had completed just days before. They were a busy couple, invested in a very full life—nothing too unusual there. But a very striking thing about Robert was the fact that he had only one leg, and he was blind.

He explained that growing up, his parents had split up, and he found himself orphaned. My heart was moved hearing him relate how as a blind, homeless teen he had stood outside houses of total strangers, hoping to be invited in for some food. To make matters worse, as an adult, Robert was accidentally run over by a car, resulting in the loss of one leg. Recovery was painful, and learning to walk with a prosthetic leg proved very challenging. "For years I was angry at God," Robert explained. "I decided that God must not exist, because no God of love could allow me to go through what I had endured." But unlike many wounded skeptics, Robert ultimately came to see that the hardships of life illustrate how desperately we *need* a Savior. "I came to trust God, I turned my heart, my belief, my emotions over to Jesus," he said. "That's when healing in my soul and blessings in my life really began."

There are many myths about Christianity in our world today. Many have believed myths that God is capricious, vindictive, uncaring, or may not even exist. We have the choice of accepting myths or rejecting them. Accepting these myths is easy; it's living differently that's difficult. Jesus did not call people to a life of ease or convenience; he called us, like Robert, to trust him to be there for us during the difficult times.

We will each leave a legacy, but what kind of legacy will it be? The legacy we leave will be based on the everyday actions we choose today, tomorrow, and the next day. When we daily choose to follow Christ, we'll find strength for today and the ability to press on during times of trials.

In our short time together in this book, I've sought to both expose the dangerous spiritual myths of our culture as well as offer helpful correctives to live according to God's truth. But I can't live a Christian life for you. Your parents can't, your spouse can't, your friends can't—only you can. Will you choose to pursue the life God has in store for you, to give you a hope and a future (Jeremiah 29:11)? My prayer is that you will.

The following pages of this book include some additional material for you to consider. If you're not sure you have a relationship with Christ or need to recommit your life to him, the next pages are for you.

In addition, several resources are available in the second appendix that I hope will continue to help you in your spiritual journey. They include free resources from my own website, additional books I have authored to help in other areas of growth, as well as information to connect with me online, or to catch my radio or television programs where you live. My goal is to help you follow God's plan for your life. Please know I am praying for you and with you to pursue his best for your future. May God bless you as you continue your journey with him!

How to Begin a Personal Relationship With Jesus Christ

People everywhere invest their lives in the search for meaning, purpose, and fulfillment. But people need something more than money, fame, luxurious houses, good looks, nice cars, or a lucrative stock portfolio. There is nothing necessarily wrong with these things, but they cannot provide peace to the soul or forgiveness of one's sin.

I once read that the highest rates of suicide and divorce occur among the most affluent classes of society. On the West Coast, psychologists and counselors have isolated a new affliction and given it a name: Sudden Wealth Syndrome. People are achieving every benchmark that our society says should make them happy, but they are finding that it is possible to be materially rich yet spiritually bankrupt. Many people have a schedule that is full but a heart that is empty.

Several years ago, our nine-member ministry team crossed America on a 50-States-in-50-Days trip. During the course of this journey, I preached in every service, in all fifty U.S. states, and personally talked with thousands of people. We had the privilege of hosting sixty-four worship services throughout the entire U.S. Our outreach team met many people who came to us with probing questions and genuine concern about spiritual issues. People today truly are looking for meaningful answers, craving hope in a dangerous world.

Present realities, such as worldwide terrorist attacks, global economic uncertainty, political instability, and natural disasters like Hurricane Katrina have only intensified this search.

Immediately after the terrorist attacks of 9/11, I went to New York City to help with a prayer center that had been set up by the Billy Graham Evangelistic Association and Samaritan's Purse. Just like on my fifty-state tour, I was talking daily to hundreds of people from every background imaginable. They may have expressed themselves in different ways, but they all had the same basic question:

"Who is God, and how may I come to know him?"

Where one stands with God is the most vital of all issues, but the good news is that you can settle this today! You may have wondered, *How does a person become a Christian? How can I be certain that my sin is forgiven? How may I experience consistent spiritual growth?* Let's consider these things together.

God's Word Explains the Message of Salvation

Jesus said in John 3:3, "No one can see the kingdom of God unless they are born again." Salvation is the issue: The most important question you will ever ask yourself is this: "Do I know for certain that I have eternal life, and that I will go to heaven when I die?"

If you stood before God right now and God asked, "Why should I let you into my heaven?" what would you say?

The Bible describes our condition: "For all have sinned and fall short of the glory of God" (Romans 3:23). Just as a job pays a wage at the end of the week, our sins will yield a result at the end of a lifetime: "For the wages of sin is death (the Bible describes this as separation from God, the punishment of hell), but the gift of God is eternal life, through Christ Jesus our Lord" (Romans 6:23).

God's love for you *personally* is shown by his provision for your need: "But God demonstrates his own love for us in this: While we were still sinners, Christ died for us" (Romans 5:8).

Salvation requires repentance, which means a "turning." Jesus said, "Unless you repent, you too will all perish" (Luke 13:3). The New Testament emphasizes the necessity of repentance and salvation: "Repent, then, and turn to God, so that your sins may be wiped out" (Acts 3:19).

Every one of us has sinned, and the Bible says that our sins must be dealt with. We have a twofold sin problem. We are sinners by birth, and we are sinners by choice. Someone once said to the great evangelist Dr. Vance Havner, "This thing about man's sin nature, I find that hard to swallow!" Dr. Havner said, "You don't have to swallow it—you're born with it, it's already in you."

The world classifies sin, viewing some things as worse than others. But the Bible teaches that all sin is an offense against God, and even one sin is serious enough to keep someone out of heaven. You may not have robbed a bank, or maybe you have. God doesn't grade on a curve; humanity is a tainted race, and sin is the problem.

Oftentimes in life we know what is right, but we do what is wrong. You may have even looked back at yourself and wondered, *What was I thinking? Why did I do that? How could I have said that?* Jesus said that people need to repent and make a change. Repentance means turning *from* your sins and *to* Christ. By faith, trust *who* Jesus is (God's Son; mankind's Savior), and *what* Jesus did (died in your place and rose from the dead).

God's forgiveness is received by faith. We are to confess our faith before others, not be ashamed to let the world know that we believe in Jesus: "That if you confess with your mouth the Lord Jesus, and believe in your heart that God has raised Him from the dead, you will be saved. For with the heart one believes unto righteousness, and with the mouth confession is made unto salvation" (Romans 10:9–10 NKJV).

What is faith? Faith is trust. It is simple, honest, childlike trust. God says that you have a sin problem, but that he loves you and will forgive you. God says that through Jesus Christ, he has made a way for anyone who will come to him to be saved. Do you trust what God has said and what God has done? If you come to Christ in belief and faith, God promises to save you: "Everyone who calls upon the name of the Lord will be saved" (Romans 10:13). Jesus promises: "Whoever comes to me I will never drive away" (John 6:37).

During the fifty-state tour, we gave away thousands of yellow stickers that said, "Jesus Saves, Pray Today!" That is not a trite saying or a marketing cliché. It is a deep biblical truth, and if you desire to have a relationship with the Lord, that can be accomplished right where you are now. Make your journey to the cross today, through this basic prayer of commitment:

Dear Lord Jesus, I know that I have sinned and I cannot save myself. I believe that you are the Son of God, and that you died and rose again for me to forgive my sins and to be my Savior. I turn from my sins and I ask you to forgive me. I receive you into my heart as my Lord and Savior. Jesus, thank you for saving me now. Help me to live the rest of my life for you. Amen.

God's Word Gives You Assurance of Salvation

You can overcome doubts about where you stand with God. Based on what God's Word says (not what you feel or assume), you can know that you have eternal life: "Whoever has the Son has life. . . . I write these things to you who believe in the name of the Son of God so that you may know that you have eternal life" (1 John 5:12–13).

Jesus said, "Whoever hears my word and believes him who sent me has eternal life and will not be judged but has crossed over from death to life" (John 5:24). Remember: You are not saved by good works, and you are not "kept saved" by good works. Your merit before God is totally based on Jesus; his perfection, holiness, and righteousness is credited to each one who believes by faith.

What Is Meant by the Term *Rededication*?

A news reporter once asked me this question. He had heard me use this term as I spoke at a church and wanted to know what I meant. Rededication is for a believer who desires that their walk with Christ be renewed and deepened. A Christian can wander from God in sin or simply lose their closeness to the Lord through the busyness of life.

A born-again Christian is forever God's child. Your salvation is a matter of *birth*. Your daily Christian growth is a matter of *fellowship*. Your spiritual birth into God's family is, in some ways, similar to your physical birth into the human family. For instance, as a child, you may have disobeyed and disappointed your father. Something you did may have grieved him, but you were still his child because you were born into that family.

In the same way, the Christian's relationship to the Lord is still intact, even though a sin we commit may hinder our daily fellowship with God. Salvation is a one-time, instantaneous event; Christian growth and personal fellowship with God are an everyday, life-long process. Consistent daily prayer, Bible study, obedience to the Holy Spirit, and nurture in a local church fellowship are all keys to growth and Christian maturity.

While your membership in the family may be intact, your daily fellowship may be lacking. Christ, not self, must be on the throne of your heart and life! Sin hinders our fellowship with God: "But your iniquities have separated you from your God; your sins have hidden his face from you, so that he will not hear" (Isaiah 59:2). Perhaps your desire is like that of David, when he wandered from God: "Create in me a pure heart, O God, and renew a steadfast spirit within me" (Psalm 51:10).

God lovingly receives all who *turn* to him, and all who *return* to him! He cleanses us from sin and restores us to fellowship with him. King David had been "a man after God's own heart," but his sinful deeds required that he humbly recommit himself to the Lord: "Do not cast me from your presence. . . . Restore to me the joy of your salvation" (Psalm 51:11–12). Christian publications often use the following verse in the context of evangelism, and that is okay, but 1 John 1:9 is really a promise to the *Christian* who needs to make things right with the Lord: "If we confess our sins, he is faithful and just and will forgive us our sins and purify us from all unrighteousness."

From the same chapter is another great truth that gives us precious, sweet assurance: "But if we walk in the light, as he is in the light, we have fellowship with one another, and the blood of Jesus, his Son, purifies us from all sin" (1 John 1:7).

You may already know the Lord but wish to pray these basic words of rededication and commitment:

Lord Jesus, I acknowledge that I have sinned and wandered from you. I confess my sin, and turn from it. I recommit myself to you as Lord. Thank you for forgiving me; I trust you to give me the strength to live for you each day of my life. Thank you for being my Savior, my Lord, and my friend. Amen.

May God bless you as you journey on with him.

If you made a decision for Christ just now, it would be an honor to hear from you. If you do not have a Bible and would like to request one, or if you have other questions or spiritual needs, write to:

Dr. Alex McFarland
viraltruth.com
PO Box 10231
Greensboro, NC 27404

Or email me through the website at alexmcfarland.com.

Appendix 2

Additional Resources

Alex's Website

Find numerous articles, Q&As, recommended resources, and information on upcoming events at alexmcfarland.com. Also connect with Alex via social media or sign up for his weekly e-news update.

Alex on Radio and Television

Listen live on American Family Radio weekdays at 4 p.m. Eastern at afr.net or on your local AFR station.

Watch Alex on the NRB television network. For times and listings, see NRBnetwork.tv.

Books by Alex McFarland

Stand: Core Truths You Must Know for an Unshakable Faith
The 10 Most Common Objections to Christianity
Stand Strong in College
Stand: Diving Into God's Words (Devotional)
Stand: Unleashing the Wisdom of God (Devotional)
Stand: Seeking the Way of God (Devotional)
10 Questions Every Christian Must Answer (coauthored with Elmer Towns)
10 Answers for Skeptics
10 Answers for Atheists
The 21 Toughest Questions Your Kids Will Ask about Christianity
10 Questions about Prayer Every Christian Must Answer (coauthored with Elmer Towns)
10 Issues That Divide Christians

Books Contributed to by Alex McFarland

Apologetics Study Bible for Students, Sean McDowell, ed. (Broadman & Holman, 2010).
Apologetics for a New Generation, Sean McDowell, ed. (Conversant Life/ Harvest House, 2009).
God in Real Life (Rose Publishing, 2009).
The Greenhouse Project: Cultivating Students of Influence, Mike Calhoun and Mel Walker, eds. (Word of Life Fellowship/Vision For Youth, February 2009).
Pushing the Limits: Unleashing the Potential of Student Ministry (Thomas Nelson, October 2006).
The Case for Christmas, Lee Strobel (Zondervan, 2005).

Appendix 3

Additional Books to Help You Investigate Faith

One book on faith can't give you all the answers you need. That's why I've included this helpful list of additional books. In some cases you'll find a brief note about the resource.

(**Please note:** The inclusion of a specific resource in this list is not intended as an endorsement of all the content available in the resource in question. As always, be discerning and, as recorded in 1 Thessalonians 5:21 (NKJV), "test all things.")

Anderson, Paul M., ed. *Professors Who Believe: The Spiritual Journeys of Christian Faculty*. Downers Grove, IL: InterVarsity Press, 1998. Several Christian professors offer reasons for their faith.

Ankerberg, John, and John Weldon. *Ready with an Answer: For the Tough Questions about God*. Eugene, OR: Harvest House, 1997. Apologists Ankerberg and Weldon offer a popular defense of Christianity, featuring questions and answers about Jesus, creation, and the Bible.

Archer, Gleason L. *Encyclopedia of Bible Difficulties*. Grand Rapids, MI: Zondervan, 1982. The go-to book for explanations of alleged discrepancies and contradictions in the Bible. Archer offers comprehensive answers to a variety of common objections Christians and non-Christians may have about difficult passages in the Bible. Arranged by the books of the Bible. See also *When Critics Ask* by Norman Geisler and Thomas Howe.

Beckwith, Francis J., and Gregory Koukl. *Relativism: Feet Firmly Planted in Mid-Air*. Grand Rapids, MI: Baker Books, 1998. Apologists Beckwith and Koukl give a devastating critique of moral relativism written in an engaging, popular style. Practical and fun to read.

Beckwith, Francis J., Carl Mosser, and Paul Owen, eds. *The New Mormon Challenge: Responding to the Latest Defenses of a Fast-Growing Movement*. Grand Rapids, MI: Zondervan, 2002. A more scholarly look than usual at the Church of Jesus Christ of Latter-Day Saints. Features a collection of essays by such Christian thinkers as William Lane Craig, Paul Copan, J. P. Moreland, Craig Blomberg, and others.

Beckwith, Francis J., William Lane Craig, and J. P. Moreland, eds. *To Everyone an Answer: A Case for the Christian Worldview*. Downers Grove, IL: InterVarsity Press, 2004. A collection of essays in honor of apologist Norman Geisler, covering many apologetics-related topics.

Behe, Michael J. *Darwin's Black Box: The Biochemical Challenge to Evolution*. New York: The Free Press, 1996. A biochemistry professor questions evolution. Some credit this book with paving the way for the rise of the Intelligent Design movement. A bit technical at times but well worth reading.

Beisner, E. Calvin. *Answers for Atheists, Agnostics, and Other Thoughtful Skeptics*. Wheaton, IL: Crossway, 1993. A look at arguments for God's existence, questions about knowledge, and evidences for Christianity.

Boa, Ken, and Larry Moody. *I'm Glad You Asked: In-Depth Answers to Difficult Questions About Christianity*. Colorado Springs, CO: Victor, 1994. An accessible book answering several questions about Christianity, including the existence of God, miracles, the Bible, evil and suffering, hypocrites in the church, salvation, and more.

Boa, Kenneth D., and Robert M. Bowman Jr. *Faith Has Its Reasons*, 2nd ed. Waynesboro, GA: Paternoster, 2005. Offers a look at four types of approaches to defending the faith, including profiles of key apologists such as C. S. Lewis. This second edition makes many improvements.

_____. *20 Compelling Evidences That God Exists: Discover Why Believing in God Makes So Much Sense*. Tulsa, OK: River Oak, 2002. The authors integrate several lines of reasoning that point to the reality of God. Some of the arguments they address include the cosmological argument, Intelligent Design issues, the Bible's reliability, fulfilled prophecy, and Jesus and his claims.

Broom, Neil. *How Blind Is the Watchmaker? Nature's Design and the Limits of Naturalistic Science*. Downers Grove, IL: InterVarsity Press, 2001. A response to Richard Dawkins's book *The Blind Watchmaker*, as well as a useful apologetic resource in its own right. Helpful in responding to proponents of scientism.

Brown, Colin. *Philosophy and the Christian Faith*. Downers Grove, IL: InterVarsity Press, 1968. Brown looks at the history of philosophy from a distinctly Christian perspective. See also Gordon Clark's *Thales to Dewey*.

Bruce, F. F. *The Defense of the Gospel in the New Testament*. Grand Rapids, MI: Eerdmans, 1977. A helpful little book documenting the extent and types of apologetics found in the pages of the New Testament.

_____. *Twenty Compelling Evidences That God Exists*. Tulsa, OK: River Oak, 2002. Presents twenty arguments for God's existence, including standard natural theology arguments, as well as specific arguments for Christ and Christianity (the resurrection, prophecy, etc.).

Budziszewski, J. *Written on the Heart: The Case for Natural Law*. Downers Grove, IL: InterVarsity Press, 1997. Budziszewski defends natural law—the idea that morality is ingrained in human beings.

Cabal, Ted, ed. *The Apologetics Study Bible*. Nashville: Holman, 2007. A unique Bible with an apologetics emphasis. Features many notes and articles by well-known contemporary apologists. Uses the Holman Christian Standard Bible translation.

Campbell-Jack, W. C., and Gavin McGrath, eds. *New Dictionary of Christian Apologetics*. Downers Grove, IL: InterVarsity Press, 2006. Similar in scope to Geisler's *Baker Encyclopedia of Christian Apologetics*, this reference work features many contributors.

Carson, D. A. *How Long, O Lord? Reflections on Suffering and Evil*. Grand Rapids, MI: Baker Books, 1990. The title is taken from Psalm 6:3. Theologian Carson addresses the problems of evil and suffering. Rather than taking the popular free-will defense, he explores other options from a Reformed perspective. Thoughtful and pastoral.

Clark, David K., and Norman L. Geisler. *Apologetics in the New Age: A Christian Critique of Pantheism*. Grand Rapids, MI: Baker Books, 1990. Provides a detailed look at many kinds of pantheism and provides a Christian evaluation.

Clark, Gordon. *Thales to Dewey*. Unicoi, TN: The Trinity Foundation, 2000. A reissue of Clark's classic 1957 textbook on philosophy, written from a Christian perspective. Clark (a presuppositional apologist) capably tackles the history of philosophy. Witty and challenging.

Clark, Kelly James, ed. *Philosophers Who Believe: The Spiritual Journeys of 11 Leading Thinkers*. Downers Grove, IL: InterVarsity Press, 1993. Like *Professors Who Believe*, but this time the testimonies are from Christian philosophers.

Copan, Paul. *Is God a Moral Monster? Making Sense of the Old Testament God*. Grand Rapids, MI: Baker Books, 2011. Christian philosopher Copan explains and defends God against the accusations of several new atheists.

Corduan, Winfried. *Neighboring Faiths: A Christian Introduction to World Religions*. Downers Grove, IL: InterVarsity Press, 1998. Corduan offers a helpful Christian overview of many religions, including their history, beliefs, and Christian responses.

_____. *No Doubt About It: The Case for Christianity.* Nashville: Broadman & Holman, 1997. This book provides a great introduction to apologetics that is both thoughtful and accessible to the layperson.

Cowan, Steven B., ed. *Five Views on Apologetics.* Grand Rapids, MI: Zondervan, 2000. Similar to Boa and Bowman's *Faith Has Its Reasons*, this work looks at five approaches to apologetics.

Craig, William Lane. *Reasonable Faith: Christian Truth and Apologetics,* 3rd ed. Wheaton, IL: Crossway Books, 2008. Craig is a top-notch philosopher and it shows in this thought-provoking apologetics book. Some portions are challenging, so consider this an option for intermediate to advanced apologists.

Craig, William Lane, and Chad Meister, eds. *God Is Great, God Is Good: Why Believing in God Is Reasonable and Responsible.* Downers Grove, IL: InterVarsity Press, 2009. This anthology includes essays responding to the new atheism.

Craig, William Lane, and Walter Sinnot-Armstrong. *God? A Debate Between a Christian and an Atheist.* New York: Oxford University Press, 2004. If you want to see apologetics in action, this is a great resource featuring one of Christianity's best debaters on the existence of God (Craig). Be prepared to confront some serious challenges from atheist Sinnott-Armstrong.

Dembski, William. *The Design Inference.* New York: Cambridge University Press, 1998. An intermediate to advanced overview of Intelligent Design by a key proponent.

Dembski, William A., and James M. Kushiner, eds. *Signs of Intelligence: Understanding Intelligent Design.* Grand Rapids, MI: Brazos Press, 2001. A collection of essays explaining and defending Intelligent Design. Contributors include individuals such as Philip E. Johnson, Nancy Pearcey, Jay Richards, Michael Behe, Jonathan Wells, and others.

D'Souza, Dinesh. *What's So Great About Christianity?* Carol Stream, IL: Tyndale House, 2008. A fun read that offers evidence for Christianity and responds to some typical criticisms of it.

Evans, C. Stephen. *Existentialism: The Philosophy of Despair and the Quest for Hope.* Dallas: Probe Books, 1984. Christian philosopher Evans tackles the worldview of despair, existentialism, and the nihilism it entails. Thoughtful and well written.

France, R. T. *The Evidence for Jesus.* Downers Grove, IL: InterVarsity Press, 1986. A good one-stop resource for evidence supporting the historical Jesus.

Geisler, Norman L. *Baker Encyclopedia of Christian Apologetics.* Grand Rapids, MI: Baker Books, 1999. This resource provides a great synthesis of the apologetics ideas of Geisler, summarizing many key topics, people, and arguments.

_____. *Christian Apologetics*. Grand Rapids, MI: Baker Books, 1976. Geisler's classic apologetics textbook. Intended for classroom use, this book contains some material that is intermediate to advanced.

_____. *The Roots of Evil*. Eugene, OR: Wipf and Stock, 1978. Geisler's short book grappling with the problem of evil and various proposed solutions.

Geisler, Norman, and Peter Bocchino. *Unshakable Foundations: Contemporary Answers to Crucial Questions About the Christian Faith*. Minneapolis: Bethany House, 2001. The authors set the foundation for logical reasoning, present and defend the meaning of truth, evaluate worldviews, look at Christianity in relation to science, and more. Also includes chapters on morality, Jesus, heaven, and hell.

Geisler, Norman L., and Ronald M. Brooks. *Come, Let Us Reason: An Introduction to Logical Thinking*. Grand Rapids, MI: Baker Books, 1990. Geisler and Brooks offer an introduction to logic that includes Christian examples. See also their book *When Skeptics Ask*.

_____. *When Skeptics Ask*. Wheaton, IL: Scripture Press, 1990. One of the best entry-level introductions to apologetics available, especially for those who prefer the classical apologetics approach. The simple and straightforward text presents powerful, concise arguments for Christianity. Highly readable.

Geisler, Norman L., and Winfried Corduan. *Philosophy of Religion*. Grand Rapids, MI: Baker Books, 1988. A somewhat academic look at philosophy of religion written by two Christian apologists. Covers God and experience, reason, language, and evil.

Geisler, Norman L., and Paul D. Feinberg. *Introduction to Philosophy: A Christian Perspective*. Grand Rapids, MI: Baker Books, 1990. An introductory philosophy textbook written from a Christian perspective. Covers key philosophy areas such as epistemology (knowledge), ultimate reality (metaphysics), and ethics.

Geisler, Norman L., and Paul K. Hoffman, eds. *Why I Am a Christian: Leading Thinkers Explain Why They Believe*, rev. and exp. ed. Grand Rapids, MI: Baker Books, 2006. A collection of thoughtful Christian testimonies that offer quite a contrast to Bertrand Russell's famous work *Why I Am Not a Christian*.

Geisler, Norman, and Thomas Howe. *When Critics Ask: A Popular Handbook of Bible Difficulties*. Wheaton, IL: Victor Books, 1992. Less academic than *Encyclopedia of Bible Difficulties* by Gleason Archer, but still thoughtful and highly accessible. Organized by the books of the Bible. The authors offer succinct but logically clear responses to common Bible difficulties.

Geisler, Norman, Alex McFarland, and Robert Velarde. *10 Questions and Answers on Atheism and Agnosticism*. Torrance, CA: Rose Publishing, 2007. This eye-catching pamphlet explores arguments for God's existence and responds to some common objections.

Geisler, Norman, and Frank Turek. *I Don't Have Enough Faith to Be an Atheist*. Wheaton, IL: Crossway Books, 2004. Geisler and Turek offer a strong defense of Christianity and also show deficiencies in atheism.

Geisler, Norman, and Patrick Zukeran. *The Apologetics of Jesus: A Caring Approach to Dealing with Doubters.* Grand Rapids, MI: Baker Books, 2009. Want to know how Jesus defended the faith? This book is the place to go.

Greenleaf, Simon. *The Testimony of the Evangelists: The Gospels Examined by the Rules of Evidence.* Grand Rapids, MI: Kregel, 1995. A reissue of a nineteenth-century work examining the key claims of Christianity on the basis of legal procedures. Short but interesting.

Groothuis, Douglas. *Christian Apologetics: A Comprehensive Case for Biblical Faith.* Downers Grove, IL: IVP Academic, 2011. Be prepared to think. Denver Seminary professor Groothuis gets into some deep apologetics issues. This is challenging material for intermediate to advanced thinkers.

_____. *Truth Decay: Defending Christianity Against the Challenges of Postmodernism.* Downers Grove, IL: InterVarsity Press, 2000. A thoughtful and even-handed analysis of postmodernism. Includes an excellent chapter on the biblical view of truth.

_____. *Unmasking the New Age: Is There a New Religious Movement Trying to Transform Society?* Downers Grove, IL: InterVarsity Press, 1986. Probably the best evangelical assessment of the New Age movement in its day. Many of the topics remain relevant and are presented in a thoughtful but readable manner.

Habermas, Gary, and Michael Licona. *The Case for the Resurrection of Jesus.* Grand Rapids, MI: Kregel, 2004. A look at the compelling evidence in favor of the resurrection of Jesus, including responses to popular rebuttals.

Hart, David Bentley. *Atheist Delusions: The Christian Revolution and Its Fashionable Enemies.* New Haven, CT: Yale University Press, 2009. An advanced response to the New Atheism by a thoughtful theology professor.

House, H. Wayne, and Joseph M. Holden. *Charts of Apologetics and Christian Evidences.* Grand Rapids, MI: Zondervan, 2006. House and Holden provide a number of apologetics-oriented charts covering arguments for God, worldviews, philosophy, religions, and more.

Kaiser, Walter C., ed. *The Archaeological Study Bible.* Grand Rapids, MI: Zondervan, 2006. A beautifully illustrated study Bible focusing on the archaeological evidence for Christianity. Includes many articles and notes of interest. NIV (1984) translation.

Keller, Timothy. *The Reason for God: Belief in an Age of Skepticism.* New York: Dutton, 2008. A robust response to New Atheists and their popular arguments.

Kennedy, D. James, and Jerry Newcombe. *What If Jesus Had Never Been Born?* Nashville: Thomas Nelson, 1994. Jerry Newcombe and the late D. James Kennedy show the many positive contributions Christianity has made.

Koukl, Greg. *Tactics: A Game Plan for Discussing Your Christian Convictions.* Grand Rapids, MI: Zondervan, 2009. A handy little book with practical tips for having conversations with non-Christians.

Kreeft, Peter. *Christianity for Modern Pagans.* San Francisco: Ignatius, 1993. Catholic apologist Peter Kreeft explores the thought-provoking writings of Blaise Pascal, presenting and commenting on them in a way that is appealing to modern, seeking individuals. See also *Making Sense of It All* by Thomas Morris.

Kreeft, Peter, and Ronald K. Tacelli. *Handbook of Christian Apologetics.* Downers Grove, IL: InterVarsity Press, 1994. A thorough and readable introduction to apologetics that covers a lot of ground. The chapter on twenty arguments for God is excellent. There's also an abridged pocket version, also published by InterVarsity.

Lewis, C. S. *Mere Christianity.* New York: Macmillan, 1952. One of C. S. Lewis's most well-known works. Book 1 offers an accessible moral argument for God's existence.

_____. *The Problem of Pain.* New York: Macmillan, 1943. Lewis tackles the problem of evil, favoring the free-will defense as the best solution.

McCallum, Dennis, ed. *The Death of Truth.* Minneapolis, MN: Bethany House, 1996. A collection of essays evaluating postmodernism's view of truth from an evangelical Christian perspective.

McDowell, Josh. *More Than a Carpenter.* Wheaton, IL: Tyndale, 1977. A true modern classic apologetics book by apologist Josh McDowell. Short and readable, the book defends the reliability of the New Testament and explores the options regarding the person of Christ.

_____. *The New Evidence That Demands a Verdict.* Nashville, TN: Thomas Nelson, 1999. What used to be two volumes originally published in the early 1970s is now an updated one-volume apologetics book. McDowell covers many topics and includes a number of quotations about Christ and Christianity.

McDowell, Josh, and Bob Hostetler. *Beyond Belief to Convictions.* Wheaton, IL: Tyndale, 2002. A look at the Christian worldview and apologetics issues specifically in reference to helping Christian young people stay strong in their faith.

McDowell, Josh, and Bill Wilson. *He Walked Among Us: Evidence for the Historical Jesus.* San Bernardino, CA: Here's Life Publishers, 1988. A defense of the historicity of Jesus, including a look at the reliability of the New Testament, non-Christian evidence for Jesus, miracles, archaeology, and other topics.

McGrath, Alister. *The Twilight of Atheism: The Rise and Fall of Disbelief in the Modern World.* New York: Doubleday, 2004. McGrath offers unique insights on atheism and the ongoing thriving of religion despite its critics.

McGrath, Alister, and Joanna Collicutt McGrath. *The Dawkins Delusion? Atheist Fundamentalism and the Denial of the Divine.* Downers Grove, IL: InterVarsity Press, 2007. Oxford scholar and his wife, Joanna, take on the challenges posed by atheist Richard Dawkins, including questions about God as a delusion, science and faith, and whether or not religion is really harmful.

Meyer, Stephen. *Signature in the Cell: DNA and the Evidence for Intelligent Design*. San Francisco: HarperOne, 2009. Christian and Intelligent Design proponent Stephen Meyer explores the scientific evidence for design in the cell.

Miller, Elliot. *A Crash Course on the New Age Movement: Describing and Evaluating a Growing Social Force*. Grand Rapids, MI: Baker Books, 1989. The editor of *Christian Research Journal* shares his testimony as a former New Age adherent and adds a sweeping overview of the movement in the late 1980s.

Montgomery, John Warwick. *History and Christianity: A Vigorous, Convincing Presentation of the Evidence for a Historical Jesus*. Minneapolis, MN: Bethany House, 1964. Featuring a foreword by C. S. Lewis, no less, this somewhat dated look at the evidence for the New Testament and Jesus remains an engaging and interesting read. Short and to the point.

Moreland, J. P. *Christianity and the Nature of Science: A Philosophical Investigation*. Grand Rapids, MI: Baker Books, 1989. A thoughtful Christian philosopher with a background in science explores questions about science and faith. Helpful for understanding the philosophy of science, as well as the limits of science (as opposed to scientism).

_____. *Love Your God with All Your Mind: The Role of Reason in the Life of the Soul*. Colorado Springs: NavPress, 1997. How does the intellectual life fit with Christianity? Moreland shows how valuable it is to use our mind in relation to our faith.

_____. *Scaling the Secular City*. Grand Rapids, MI: Baker Books, 1987. A strong intermediate introduction to apologetics. Moreland is particularly good at looking at the relationship between faith and science.

Moreland, J. P., and William Lane Craig. *Philosophical Foundations for a Christian Worldview*. Downers Grove, IL: InterVarsity Press, 2003. This tome is meant as a textbook and it shows; best for intermediate to advanced apologists. Moreland and Craig are two top contemporary apologists.

Moreland, J. P., and Kai Nielsen. *Does God Exist? The Great Debate*. Nashville: Thomas Nelson, 1990. Moreland represents Christianity well in this helpful debate on the existence of God.

Morgan, Christopher W., and Robert A. Peterson, eds. *Faith Comes by Hearing: A Response to Inclusivism*. Downers Grove, IL: IVP Academic, 2008. An academic defense of Christian exclusivism claims, featuring a number of contributors. Helpful in relation to inclusivism (the view that God may save those who are not explicitly Christian), as well as in relation to religious pluralism (see the glossary).

Morison, Frank. *Who Moved the Stone?* Grand Rapids, MI: Zondervan, 1976. A reissue of a 1930s book that asks a seemingly simple question about the resurrection of Jesus and builds a strong apologetic case for it.

Morris, Thomas V. *Making Sense of It All: Pascal and the Meaning of Life*. Grand Rapids, MI: William B. Eerdmans Publishing Company, 1992. May appeal to thoughtful and seeking skeptics, agnostics, and nihilists who are seeking real meaning in life. Morris weaves in the philosophy of Christian philosopher and scientist Blaise Pascal, noting how relevant his insights remain even in our modern day. See also *Christianity for Modern Pagans* by Peter Kreeft.

Muncaster, Ralph O. *Evidence for Jesus: Discover the Facts That Prove the Truth of the Bible*. Eugene, OR: Harvest House, 2004. A popular and readable overview of the evidence for Jesus, covering manuscript evidence, the resurrection, archaeology, prophecies, and more.

Netland, Harold. *Encountering Religious Pluralism: The Challenge to Christian Faith and Mission*. Downers Grove, IL: InterVarsity Press, 2001. An intermediate to advanced work evaluating sophisticated forms of religious pluralism and offering Christian insights to help engage those beliefs. Thoughtful, challenging reading. The chapter on an evangelical theology of religions is excellent.

Noebel, David A. *Understanding the Times: The Collision of Today's Competing Worldviews*. Manitou Springs, CO: Summit Press, 2006. An abridged version of David Noebel's thoughtful look at various worldviews, such as secular humanism, Marxism, cosmic humanist theology, and biblical Christianity. Specifically looks at theology, philosophy, ethics, biology, psychology, sociology, law, politics, economics, and history.

Orr-Ewing, Amy. *Is Believing in God Irrational?* Downers Grove, IL: InterVarsity Press, 2008. A short work answering several challenges to the faith, including questions about truth, hell, religious experience, and more.

Pearcey, Nancy. *Total Truth: Liberating Christianity from Its Cultural Captivity*. Wheaton, IL: Crossway Books, 2004. A former student of the late Francis Schaeffer, Pearcey presents a thorough look at the Christian worldview and how it relates to all of life. Not overtly apologetic in nature, but it does touch on important issues related to apologetics.

Rhodes, Ron. *Answering the Objections of Atheists, Agnostics, and Skeptics*. Eugene , OR: Harvest House, 2006. A helpful popular-level book responding to atheism, agnosticism, and skepticism.

_____. *The Complete Book of Bible Answers: Answering the Tough Questions*. Eugene, OR: Harvest House, 1997. Popular apologist and theologian Ron Rhodes takes on common questions and objections about the Bible. Covers the reliability of the Bible, Jesus, ethics, apologetics issues, and more.

_____. *The Counterfeit Christ of the New Age Movement*. Grand Rapids, MI: Baker Books, 1990. One of the best evangelical assessments of the New Age view of Jesus. Rhodes responds to claims about the so-called lost years of Jesus, as well as to common New Age views of Jesus. He closes with powerful chapters about the real, biblical Jesus and his claims on our lives.

Samples, Kenneth Richard. *Without a Doubt: Answering the 20 Toughest Faith Questions*. Grand Rapids, MI: Baker Books, 2004. Tackles several apologetics issues including the existence of God.

Schmidt, Alvin J. *How Christianity Changed the World.* Grand Rapids, MI: Zondervan, 2004. A lengthy look at areas where Christianity has benefitted the world. Well-researched and documented.

Sennett, James F., and Douglas Groothuis, eds. *In Defense of Natural Theology: A Post-Humean Assessment.* Downers Grove, IL: InterVarsity Press, 2005. A somewhat academic work featuring a collection of essays by Christians defending natural theology arguments such as the cosmological argument, the moral argument, and other topics.

Sire, James. *Habits of the Mind: Intellectual Life as a Christian Calling.* Downers Grove, IL: InterVarsity Press, 2000. Sire looks at the importance of the intellectual life in the Christian worldview. See also J. P. Moreland's Love *Your God With All Your Mind.*

———. *A Little Primer on Humble Apologetics.* Downers Grove, IL: InterVarsity Press, 2006. Offers practical advice for budding apologists, including insights on the importance of character.

———. *The Universe Next Door: A Basic Worldview Catalog,* 5th ed. Downers Grove, IL: InterVarsity Press, 2009 . This is one of the go-to books on understanding worldviews from a Christian perspective.

———. *Why Should Anyone Believe Anything at All?* Downers Grove, IL: InterVarsity Press, 1994. James Sire explores reasons people believe or don't believe. In the process he discusses apologetics issues including Jesus, evil and suffering, the resurrection, the reliability of the Gospels, and several other engaging topics.

Story, Dan. *Engaging the Closed Minded: Presenting Your Faith to the Confirmed Unbeliever.* Grand Rapids, MI: Kregel, 1999. Offers helpful observations about witnessing to non-Christians.

Strobel, Lee. *The Case for a Creator: A Journalist Investigates Scientific Evidence That Points Toward God.* Grand Rapids, MI: Zondervan, 2004. Strobel turns his journalistic style to the topic of science. He interviews a number of scholars and scientists on topics such as evolution, faith and science, the cosmological argument, fine-tuning (design) arguments for God, human consciousness, and more.

———. *The Case for Christ: A Journalist's Personal Investigation of the Evidence for Jesus.* Grand Rapids, MI: Zondervan, 1998. Strobel's highly readable and moving book featuring interviews with scholars regarding the person of Christ. Covers the reliability of the New Testament Gospels, non-Christian evidence for Jesus, scientific evidence, the case for the resurrection, and more.

———. *The Case for Faith: A Journalist Investigates the Toughest Objections to Christianity.* Grand Rapids, MI: Zondervan, 2000. Strobel continues with his journalistic interview style, this time exploring eight popular objections to Christianity, such as evil and suffering, evolution, hell, miracles, and more.

Swinburne, Richard. *Is There a God?* New York: Oxford University Press, 1996. A thoughtful Christian philosopher of religion makes the case for God and responds to the problem of evil.

Taylor, James E. *Introducing Apologetics: Cultivating Christian Commitment.* Grand Rapids, MI: Baker Books, 2006. An introductory apologetics textbook covering many key issues, including worldviews, science and faith, the problem of evil, moral relativism, Jesus, and other matters. Includes chapter summaries, reflection and discussion questions, and suggestions for further reading at the end of each chapter.

Velarde, Robert. *Conversations with C. S. Lewis: Imaginative Discussions About Life, Christianity, and God.* Downers Grove, IL: InterVarsity Press, 2008. A fun read featuring fictional discussions between C. S. Lewis and a skeptic. Covers a lot of apologetic ground, including arguments for God's existence. Suitable for an open-minded skeptic or for the edification of Christians.

Wells, Jonathan. *Icons of Evolution: Science or Myth? Why Much of What We Teach About Evolution Is Wrong.* Washington, DC: Regnery Publishing, 2000. In this work, later made into a documentary of the same main title, Wells takes on many misconceptions meant to support evolution that fail. Included topics cover the experiment that supposedly created life in the laboratory, Darwin's tree of life, Haeckel's embryo drawings, peppered moths, archaeopteryx, Darwin's finches, and human evolution.

Wilkens, Steve. *Good Ideas from Questionable Christians and Outright Pagans: An Introduction to Key Thinkers and Philosophers.* Downers Grove, IL: InterVarsity Press, 2004. A helpful Christian introduction to philosophy, covering thinkers such as Socrates, Plato, Aristotle, Augustine, Aquinas, Descartes, Kierkegaard, Nietzsche, and others.

Notes

Introduction

1. Alex McFarland, *The 10 Most Common Objections to Christianity* (Ventura, CA: Regal, 2007), 210–211.

Myth #1

1. Mahatma Gandhi quoted in *Famous Quotes from 100 Great People* (Mobile Reference, Google eBook, 2011).

2. Alex McFarland, *The 21 Toughest Questions Your Children Will Ask About Christianity* (Carol Stream, IL: Tyndale, 2014), 213.

3. Bruce Sheiman, *An Atheist Defends Religion: Why Humanity Is Better Off With Religion Than Without It* (New York: Penguin, 2009), xiii.

4. Jonathan Falwell, quoted in Macel Falwell, *Falwell: His Life and Legacy* (New York: Howard and Simon and Schuster, 2008), 178.

Myth #2

1. Winfried Corduan, *No Doubt About It: The Case for Christianity* (Nashville: Broadman and Holman Publishers, 1997), 132.

2. C. S. Lewis, *The Problem of Pain* (San Francisco: Harper San Francisco, 2001), 93.

Myth #3

1. Gary R. Habermas and Michael R. Licona, *The Case for the Resurrection of Jesus* (Grand Rapids, MI: Kregel, 2004).

2. D. G. Dunn, *The Evidence for Jesus* (Louisville, KY: Westminster, 1985), 68.

3. Quoted in Louis Cassels, *The Reality of God* (Scottsdale, PA: Herald Press, 1972).

4. Ibid.

Myth #4

1. William A. Dembski, *Intelligent Design: The Bridge Between Science and Theology* (Downers Grove, IL: InterVarsity Press, 1999), 110.

2. Stephen C. Meyer, *Signature in the Cell* (San Francisco: HarperOne, 2010), introduction.

3. For more on this area, see my coauthored book with Elmer Towns, *10 Questions Every Christian Must Answer: Thoughtful Responses to Strengthen Your Faith* (Nashville: B&H Publishing, 2011), chapter 3.

4. G. Gamow, "Broadening Horizons," in *The World of Physics: A Small Library of the Literature of Physics from Antiquity to the Present* (New York: Simon and Schuster, 1987), 3:259.

5. Norman Geisler and Jason Jimenez, *The Bible's Answers to 100 of Life's Biggest Questions* (Grand Rapids, MI: Baker Books, 2015), 41–42.

6. Richard Dawkins, *River Out of Eden: A Darwinian View of Life* (New York: Basic Books, 1995), 131–132.

7. Hugh Ross and Fazale Rana, *Who Was Adam?* (Colorado Springs: Navpress, 2005), 248–250.

8. William Dembski, PhD, spoken in a roundtable discussion on origins, "Defending the Faith, Defending the Family" conference, Northside Baptist Church, Charlotte, NC, October 15, 2010. Roundtable moderated by Alex McFarland.

9. Stephen C. Meyer, "A Scientific History—and Philosophical Defense—of the Theory of Intelligent Design." Discovery Institute, 2004, 29, www.discovery.org/a/7471.

Myth #5

1. Michael Stone, "Study shows religious people are less intelligent than non-believers," Examiner.com, August 13, 2013, www.examiner.com/article/study-shows-religious-people-are-less-intelligent-than-non-believers.

2. J. Warner Wallace, "About the Author," Cold-Case Christianity, http://coldcasechristianity.com/j-warner-wallace-christian-apologist-and-author/. See also J. Warner Wallace, *Cold-Case Christianity* (Colorado Springs: David C. Cook, 2013).

3. Frank Morison, *Who Moved the Stone?* (Grand Rapids, MI: Zondervan, 2002), 193.

4. C. S. Lewis, *Surprised by Joy* (New York: Harcourt, Brace & World, Inc., 1955), 175, 191.

5. Ibid., 228–229.

6. Josh McDowell, *Evidence that Demands a Verdict,* 373. As cited in John Ankerberg and John Weldon, "The Evidence for the Resurrection," www.jashow.org/wiki/index.php?title=The_Evidence_for_the_Resurrection_of_Jesus_Christ/Part_1.

7. The John Ankerberg Show, transcript of a debate between Dr. John Warwick Montgomery and John K. Naland, televised April 1990, 39.

8. Ibid.

9. Malcolm Muggeridge, *Jesus: The Man Who Lives* (New York: Harper & Row, 1978), 7, 184, 191.

10. Some information in this section has been adapted from John Ankerberg and John Weldon, "The Evidence for the Resurrection," www.jashow.org/wiki/index.php?title=The_Evidence_for_the_Resurrection_of_Jesus_Christ/Part_1. Used with permission.

11. St. Thomas Aquinas, quoted in Peter Kreeft, *The Philosophy of St. Thomas Aquinas* (Boston: Recorded Books, 2009), 13.

12. Norman Geisler and Jason Jimenez, *The Bible's Answers to 100 of Life's Biggest Questions* (Grand Rapids, MI: Baker Books, 2015), 18.

Myth #6

1. Dillon Burroughs, *Undefending Christianity: Embracing Truth Without Having All the Answers* (Eugene, OR: Harvest House Publishers, 2011), 86.

2. Billy Graham, as cited at http://billygraham.org/story/billy-graham-quotes-on-heaven.

3. Sam Storms, "Heaven: The Eternal Increase of Joy," *Decision Magazine*, April 2007, http://billygraham.org/decision-magazine/april-2007/heaven-the-eternal-increase-of-joy.

4. Randy Alcorn, *Heaven* (Carol Stream, IL: Tyndale, 2011), 160.

Myth #7

1. Stephanie's story is taken from Alex McFarland and Elmer Towns, *10 Questions Every Christian Must Answer: Thoughtful Responses to Strengthen Your Faith* (Nashville: B&H Publishing, 2014), 189–191.

2. Dayna Drum, "It's Time to Address Spiritual Abuse in the Church," *Relevant Magazine*, October 27, 2014, www.relevantmagazine.com/god/church/its-time-address-spiritual-abuse-church.

3. Alex McFarland, *10 Answers for Skeptics* (Ventura, CA: Regal, 2011), 59.

4. Daniel Sherman, "Pastoral Burnout: The Silent Ministry Killer," www.pastorburnout.com.

5. Dillon Burroughs and Marla Alupoaicei, *Generation Hex: Understanding the Subtle Dangers of Wicca* (Eugene, OR: Harvest House Publishers, 2008), 103.

6. Actual church name changed. McFarland, *10 Answers for Skeptics*, 63.

7. Joe Carter, "When Atheists Are Angry," *First Things*, January 12, 2011. Accessed at http://www.firstthings.com/web-exclusives/2011/01/when-atheists-are-angry-at-god.

8. Mary DeMuth, "Spiritual Abuse: 10 Ways to Spot It," September 29, 2011, www.marydemuth.com/spiritual-abuse-10-ways-to-spot-it.

Myth #8

1. Bart Ehrman, *Forged: Writing in the Name of God* (San Francisco: HarperOne, 2011), introduction.

2. Peter W. Stoner and Robert C. Newman, *Science Speaks* (Chicago: Moody Press, 1976).

3. A criticism sometimes leveled against the Bible is that it teaches *geocentrism* (belief that the earth is the center of the solar system, a theory taught by

Ptolemaeus, AD 90–168). But the fact is that Ptolemy's geocentrism was more influenced by Aristotle than by Scripture. Criticisms about the Bible's supposed scientific errors are also raised regarding verses such as Ecclesiastes 1:5, which speaks of the sun rising. Norman Geisler says it well by pointing out that the Bible writers' "use of observational, nonscientific language is not *un*-scientific, it is merely *pre*-scientific" (Norman L. Geisler and Thomas Howe, *When Critics Ask* [Wheaton, IL: Victor, 1992], 18). The Bible is accurate when it addresses the earth and physical phenomena, but it uses nontechnical, everyday language. For further reading on the topic of alleged scientific errors in Scripture, the author suggests Lee Strobel, *The Case for a Creator* (Grand Rapids, MI: Zondervan, 2005).

4. Millar Burrows, *More Light on the Dead Sea Scrolls* (New York: Viking Press, 1958), 81.

5. McFarland, *The 21 Toughest Questions Your Children Will Ask About Christianity*, chapter 17.

6. Gleason Archer, *Encyclopedia of Bible Difficulties* (Grand Rapids, MI: Zondervan, 1982), 11–12.

Myth #9

1. Rudolf Bultmann, *Jesus and the Word* (London: Collins/Fontana, 1958), 13.

Myth #10

1. Rob Bell, *Love Wins* (San Francisco: HarperOne, 2011), preface.

2. The following three paragraphs are from Alex McFarland and Elmer Towns, *10 Questions Every Christian Must Answer* (Nashville: B&H Publishing, 2011), 131.

3. R. W. Yarbrough, "Jesus on Hell," in *Hell Under Fire*, eds. C. W. Morgan and R. A. Peterson (Grand Rapids, MI: Zondervan, 2004), 79.

4. Ibid., 80.

5. Bell, *Love Wins*, 2–3.

6. Don Richardson, *Eternity in Their Hearts* (Minneapolis, MN: Bethany House, 2006).

7. C. S. Lewis, *Mere Christianity* (New York: Macmillan Publishing, 1952), 65.

8. C. S. Lewis, *The Screwtape Letters* (New York: HarperCollins, 2001), 47.

As a speaker, writer, and advocate for apologetics, **Alex McFarland** has spoken in hundreds of locations throughout the U.S. and abroad. He has preached in over 1,500 different churches throughout North America and internationally,  and has been featured at conferences such as the Billy Graham School of Evangelism, Focus on the Family's *Big Dig,* Josh McDowell's *True Foundations* events, California's *Spirit West Coast,* and many more.

He has been interviewed on *Fox and Friends* (the most widely watched morning show in the U.S.), the *Alan Colmes Show,* Fox News' *The Strategy Room,* NPR's *All Things Considered, The New York Times, The Washington Post,* Chuck Colson's *Breakpoint* broadcast, CBS, FOX, NBC News, the Associated Press, *LA Times, Boston Herald,* and numerous other media outlets. In a 2009 story, CNN called Alex McFarland "an expert on world religions and cults."

During the 1990s (at a time when it was predicted that the need for apologetics was waning), Alex pioneered apologetics conferences designed to equip teens and adults to defend their faith. Attendees of all ages attended the Truth for a New Generation and National Conference on Christian Apologetics events, eagerly learning from scholars such as Josh McDowell, Ravi Zacharias, Lee Strobel, and others.

Alex served as Focus on the Family's first-ever director of Teen Apologetics, then went on to serve as president of Southern Evangelical Seminary in Charlotte, North Carolina. He was named one of the "Forty Leaders Under the Age of Forty" by the North Carolina Jaycees. Alex is the only evangelist known to have preached in all fifty states in only fifty days, through his Tour of Truth. This speaking tour included sixty-four evangelistic services, became the subject of Alex's first book, and was used by God to bring many people to personal faith in Christ.

Alex developed and hosted three nationally syndicated radio broadcasts; *Exploring the Word* (co-hosted with Rev. Bert Harper) is heard weekdays in two hundred markets served by the American Family Radio Network (www.afa.net).

Alex and ministry colleague Jason Jimenez are seen weekly via the NRB television network on *Viral Truth,* a half-hour apologetics program aimed at reaching millennials and younger with the Christian message. Alex and Jason's broadcasting and speaking schedules may be followed at: www.standstrongtour.com and www.viraltruth.com.

As a broadcaster, Alex provides on-air teaching, fields live questions from listeners, and has interviewed hundreds of notable guests, including a variety of Christian leaders (e.g., James Dobson, Chuck Colson, George Barna, Tony Campolo, Ravi Zacharias, and Franklin Graham); political newsmakers (e.g., Mike Huckabee, Michele Bachmann, Rick Santorum, Maggie Gallagher, and Judge Roy Moore); skeptics (e.g., Christopher Hitchens, Michael Shermer); and musicians (e.g., Brian Wilson of The Beach Boys, and Grammy winners Marilyn McCoo and Billy Davis Jr.).

As an author, Alex McFarland has written over 150 published articles and is the author of many books, including *The 10 Most Common Objections to Christianity* (Regal) and the

STAND series, including *Stand Strong in College* (Focus on the Family/Tyndale).

Alex McFarland attended the University of North Carolina at Greensboro and earned a Master's degree in Christian Thought/Apologetics from Liberty University. He was awarded an honorary Doctor of Divinity degree by Southern Evangelical Seminary in 2006. In 2009, Alex studied further in the program *Developing Young Leaders In Higher Education*—an invitation-only study program at Harvard University. In May 2014, McFarland was awarded an honorary Doctor of Letters degree by Louisiana Baptist University.

Angie McFarland is the godly and supportive wife who has played a tremendous role in all that the Lord has called Alex to do. They have been married since 1988 and live in North Carolina.

More From
Alex McFarland

Have you ever been confronted about your beliefs and not known how to respond? Here, Alex McFarland prepares you for this uncomfortable eventuality, offering straight answers to ten common objections to Christianity. With knowledge and confidence, you can avoid a crisis of faith.

The 10 Most Common Objections to Christianity

Today's skeptics are looking for authenticity, integrity, and straightforward truth. In this book, you'll learn how to answer intimidating questions, identify the root issue behind those questions, and dismantle the "spiritual bombshells" dropped by nonbelievers.

10 Answers for Skeptics

Learn how to have an intelligent conversation about the existence of God with a nonbeliever! This unique resource exposes the philosophical assumptions at the root of atheism and exposes the fallacies that perpetuate unbelief. With the easy-to-understand charts, clear explanations, and biblical answers in this book, you'll be ready to engage in thoughtful discussions about faith.

10 Answers for Atheists

⬧ BETHANY HOUSE

Stay up-to-date on your favorite books and authors with our free e-newsletters. Sign up today at bethanyhouse.com.

Find us on Facebook. facebook.com/BHPnonfiction

Follow us on Twitter. @bethany_house